LONDON COACH

Colin Lloyd
Keith Grimes
Jef Johnson

Capital Transport

First published 1995

ISBN 185414 172 4

Published by Capital Transport Publishing
38 Long Elmes, Harrow Weald, Middlesex

Printed by Pineland Press
Hemel Hempstead, Herts

© Capital Transport Publishing 1995

The front cover and title page photographs are by Colin Lloyd

ABBEY TRAVEL 6
ALLIED (see WINGS)
AMR 6
ANDERSON 7
ANGEL MOTORS 7
APPLE COACHES 10
A&R INTERNATIONAL 10
ARMCHAIR 11
ARON COACHES 11
ASHFORD LUXURY 11
ASTONS (see BRENTS)
AVON COACHES/GATWICK FLYER 14
BANSTEAD COACHES 15
BERRYHURST 15
BEST TOURS 15
BLUEWAYS 17
BOOKHAM COACHES 18
BRENTS/ASTONS 18
BRENTONS OF BLACKHEATH 19
CAMBRIDGE COACH SERVICES 21
CAPITAL COACHES 22
CANTABRICA/LEN WRIGHT 26
CHALFONT 27
CHALFONT LINE 27
CHANNEL COACHWAYS 27
CHECKER TRAVEL 30
CHIVERS COACHES 30
CLAREMONT 30
CLARKE'S OF LONDON 31
COLLINS COACHES 34
DAVID CORBEL 34
CUMFILUX COACHES 35
DAVIAN COACHES 35
D&J COACHES 35
EBDON'S TOURS 35
P&J ELLIS 38
ENFIELDIAN 38
EMPRESS OF LONDON 39
EPSOM COACHES 39

ESCORT COACHES 42
ESSEX COACHWAYS/PATHFINDER 42
FALCON TRAVEL 43
FINCHLEY/SOUTHGATE COACHES 43
FOREST COACHES 43
FRAMES RICKARDS 46
GATWICK FLYER (see AVON)
GAYTIME 47
GOLDENSTAND 47
A. GREEN'S 47
GREEN LINE 50
GREY-GREEN 54
GUIDELINE 55
HAMILTON 55
HAMPTONS 58
HARDINGS 59
HAROLD WOOD COACHES 59
HARRIS COACHES 59
HEARN'S/VENTURE 62
HILLS OF HERSHAM 63
HOUSTON & BRYANT 63
IDEAL SERVICES 66
IMPACT 66
ISLEWORTH 67
KENTISH BUS & COACH 68
KINGS FERRY 69
LACEY'S 72
LEOLINE TRAVEL 72
LEWIS 72
LIMEBOURNE 73
LINK LINE PULLMAN 76
THE LONDONERS 76
LONDON COACHES/NORTH KENT 77
MARSHALLS 80
METROBUS 80
MITCHAM BELLE COACHES 81
NAUGHTON'S 81
NEW BHARAT COACHES 81
NORTH KENT (see LONDON COACHES)

PATHFINDER (see ESSEX COACHWAYS)
PEMICO TRAVEL 84
PRAIRIE 85
PREMIER-ALBANIAN 85
P&S TRAVEL 85
PROVENCE PRIVATE HIRE 88
R&I COACHES 88
RALPH'S COACHES 89
REDWING COACHES 92
RELIANCE OF GRAVESEND 92
PETER REYNOLDS COACHES 93
REYNOLDS DIPLOMAT 93
SSS 93
SCANCOACHES 96
SHEENWAY (see TELLINGS)
SHIRE COACHES 97
SILVERGRAY 97
SKINNERS 97
SMITH'S 100
SPEEDLINK 100
SPIRIT OF LONDON 104
STARLINE 104
STORT VALLEY 105
SUNBURY COACHES 105
SWALLOW COACH COMPANY 108
TELLINGS GOLDEN MILLER/SHEENWAY 108
EDWARD THOMAS & SON 109
THORPES 112
TIME TRAVEL 112
TRAVELLERS 113
TRINATOURS 113
VENTURE (see HEARN'S)
WESTBUS 116
WEST'S COACHES 116
WESTWAY 116
WINDSORIAN 117
WINGS EXECUTIVE/ALLIED 117
WOOLLONS COACHES 120
LEN WRIGHT (see CANTABRICA)

R & I operate a large mixed fleet with mini, midi and full size coaches as well as mini and midi-buses for LT tendered routes. One of the usual Caetano Optimo mini-coach bodied Toyota Coasters is crossing a busy Buckingham Palace Road in April 1994. *Colin Lloyd*

Marshalls acquired Ronsway of Hemel Hempstead in early 1994. D508WNV is one of the original styles of Caetano Algarve imported into Britain and was freshly painted into Marshalls colours when seen in Hemel Hempstead bus station in March 1994. This coach is the only Bedford still operated in the 25 strong fleet. *Colin Lloyd*

Anyone with £300,000 to spare could surely treat themselves to one of these superb machines, the Neoplan Spaceliner. Although similar to the Skyliner, this coach has extra stowage space on the lower deck leaving only six seats. M409TWF was seen in Hampton Court during October, the first example imported into Britain. Geoff Rixon

INTRODUCTION

Within the M25 are over 300 coach operators, large and small. This handbook is of necessity selective, but care has been taken to include the more interesting fleets and all of the larger ones. Also included are operators outside the M25 boundary who run commuter services into central London on Mondays to Fridays. Coaches in Green Line livery are also brought together in a single list. It is hoped to publish further editions at roughly two-yearly intervals and comments for the 1997 edition are welcome.

The authors and publisher would like to thank Steve Hillier, Glenn Jenkins, Keith Kiverstein, Geoff Rixon, Dave Stewart, the London Omnibus Traction Society, the PSV Circle and especially most of the operators herein for assistance during the preparation of this book. Information is correct to January 1995.

ABBEY TRAVEL

Mandy Travel Ltd, 46 Cromwell Road, London, N10 2PD

✗ACH972A	Volvo B10M-61	Jonckheere Jubilee P50	C51FT	1983	Ex Grahams, Paisley, 1985
A641VVX	Volvo B10M-61	Berkhof Esprite 350	C49FT	1983	Ex Sampson, Hoddesdon, 1993
A830NTW	Volvo B10M-61	Berkhof Esprite 350	C49FT	1983	Ex Sampson, Hoddesdon, 1993
C339UFP	Mercedes-Benz 0303	Mercedes-Benz	C49FTL	1986	Ex Abelace, Nazeing, 1994
D525BBV	Hestair Duple 425 SDA1512	Duple 425	C53FT	1987	Ex Allenways, Birmingham, 1992
E998DGS	Van Hool T815	Van Hool Acron	C49FT	1988	Ex Robins, Watton-at-Stone, 1991
J606KGB	Mercedes-Benz 609D	Dormobile Routemaker	C24F	1991	

Named Vehicle

ACH972A	Westminster	A641VVX	Woburn	E998DGS		Waltham
A830NTW	Anglesey	D525BBV	Scone			

Previous Registrations

ACH972A	ONV650Y	A641VVX	A825NTW, EBZ6531

Livery
White with blue signwriting.

AMR

AMR Transportation Services (UK) Ltd, Bedfont Trading Estate North, Bedfont Road, Feltham, TW14 8EE

VWB866Y	Bedford YMPS	Plaxton Paramount 3200	C33F	1983	Ex Angel Motors, London N15, 1989
A526LPP	Mercedes-Benz L608D	Reeve Burgess	C21F	1983	Ex Angel Motors, London N15, 1989
A528LPP	Leyland Tiger TRCTL11/3R	Plaxton Paramount 3500	C53F	1983	Ex Clarke, Burbage, 1994
A80WHS	DAF SB2300DHTD585	Plaxton Paramount 3200	C53F	1984	Ex Peacock, Locharbriggs, 1990
B126TPO	Mercedes-Benz L608D	Robin Hood	C21F	1984	Ex Angel Motors, London N15, 1989
B127TPO	Mercedes-Benz L608D	Robin Hood	C21F	1984	Ex Angel Motors, London N15, 1990
B675XTS	DAF SB2300DHS585	Plaxton Paramount 3200	C53F	1984	Ex Midland, Auchterarder, 1990
B702GJR	Volvo B10M-61	Duple Laser 2	C53F	1985	Ex Jeffs, Helmdon, 1994
B232RRU	DAF SB2300DHS585	Plaxton Paramount 3200	C53F	1985	Ex Angel Motors, London N15, 1989
B730TEL	Bedford YMPS	Plaxton Paramount 3200 II	C33F	1985	Ex Angel Motors, London N15, 1989
C795GHD	DAF SB2300DHTD585	Plaxton Paramount 3200	C53F	1985	Ex Lovering, Combe Martin, 1990
C263GMA	Mercedes-Benz L608D	PMT Hanbridge	C25F	1985	Ex Angel Motors, London N15, 1992
C283RSF	DAF MB200DKVL600	Plaxton Paramount 3500 II	C47FT	1986	Ex Wilson, Carnwath, 1994
C338UFP	Bedford YMPS	Plaxton Paramount 3200 II	C35F	1986	Ex Angel Motors, London N15, 1992
D823AUT	DAF SB2300DHS585	Duple 340	C53F	1987	Ex Angel Motors, London N15, 1994
D144HML	Mercedes-Benz 609D	Reeve Burgess	C19F	1987	Ex Angel Motors, London N15, 1994
E774MMH	Toyota Coaster HB31R	Caetano Optimo	C18F	1987	Ex Trina Tours, London WC2, 1993
E499OHD	Toyota Coaster BB30R	Caetano Optimo	C19F	1987	Ex Traject, Halifax, 1993
E863AWA	Ford Transit	Ford	M14	1988	Ex private owner, 1988
✗ GIL2781	DAF MB230DKFL615	Caetano Algarve	C53F	1988	Ex Euroline, Long Eaton, 1994
F205EWN	DAF SB2305DHS585	Caetano Algarve	C53F	1989	Ex D Coaches, Morriston, 1994
F206EWN	DAF SB2305DHS585	Caetano Algarve	C53F	1989	Ex D Coaches, Morriston, 1994
F292OTL	Freight-Rover Sherpa	Freight-Rover	B16F	1989	Ex Angel Motors, London N15, 1991
G341VHU	Leyland Swift ST2R44C97T5	Reeve Burgess Harrier	C33F	1989	Ex Compass, Childwall, 1994
G968SND	Mazda E2200	Made To Measure	M14	1989	
H261FPD	Mercedes-Benz 609D	Crystals	C23F	1991	Ex Clarkson, South Elmsall, 1993
K264PLA	Ford Transit	Ford	M14	1992	
L932TGT	DAF 400	DAF	B16F	1993	
L933TGT	DAF 400	DAF	B16F	1993	

Livery
White with blue and red relief.

Previous Registrations

GIL2781	E167KNH	B675XTS	B167SKM, 2178ND	E499OHD	E717GNH, SIB1296

ANDERSON

Anderson Travel Ltd, 178a Tower Bridge Road, London, SE1 3LS

✗ 448DAE	Mercedes-Benz 0303/15R	Jonckheere Jubilee P50	C49FT	1983	Ex Chartercoach, Dovercourt, 1993
SIJ5917	Volvo B10M-61	Jonckheere Jubilee P50	C49FT	1988	Ex Antler Holidays, Rugeley, 1991
G154XJF	DAF SB2305DHS585	Caetano Algarve	C53F	1990	
J504LRY	DAF SB3000DKV601	Caetano Algarve	C49FT	1992	
J505LRY	DAF SB3000DKV601	Caetano Algarve	C37FT	1992	
J409GFG	Leyland-DAF 410	Crystals	C16F	1992	
J528JNH	MAN 16-290	Jonckheere Deauville P599	C51FT	1992	
K212CBD	MAN 16-290HOCLR	Jonckheere Deauville P599	C53F	1993	
K213CBD	MAN 16-290HOCLR	Jonckheere Deauville P599	C51FT	1993	
K214CBD	MAN 16-290HOCLR	Jonckheere Deauville P599	C51FT	1993	
L23CAY	MAN 11-290	Caetano Algarve II	C32FT	1994	
L98RYD	Bova FHD12-340	Bova Futura	C53F	1994	
L948JFU	Mercedes-Benz 410D	Autobus Classique	C16F	1994	
M568BVL	Mercedes-Benz 814D	Autobus Classique	C25F	1994	

Previous Registrations
448DAE   From New   SIJ5917   E700NNH

Livery
White with green and black relief.

Special Livery
Evan Evans Tours (Red and cream);- K212 CBD.

ANGEL MOTORS

Angel Motors (Edmonton) Ltd, Constable Crescent, London, N15 4QZ

E835EUT	Mercedes-Benz 307D	Yeates	M12	1987	
✗ E321EVH	DAF SB2300DHS585	Plaxton Paramount 3500 III	C51FT	1987	
E344EVH	DAF SB2300DHS585	Plaxton Paramount 3500 III	C53F	1987	
E405LPR	DAF SB2305DHS585	Plaxton Paramount 3200 III	C55F	1987	
E702UND	Mercedes-Benz 609D	Made To Measure	C19F	1987	
E636KCX	DAF SB2305DHS585	Duple 340	C57F	1988	
F322SMD	Mercedes-Benz 609D	Reeve Burgess	C23F	1988	
F323SMD	Mercedes-Benz 609D	Reeve Burgess	C23F	1988	
F917YNV	Volvo B10M-60	Jonckheere Deauville P599	C49FT	1989	Ex Cross Gates, Llandrindod Wells, 1992
F647OHD	DAF SB3000DKV601	Plaxton Paramount 3500 III	C51FT	1989	
F648OHD	DAF SB3000DKV601	Plaxton Paramount 3500 III	C51FT	1989	
G264EHD	DAF SB2305DHS585	Van Hool Alizee	C55F	1989	Ex Palmer, Normanton, 1992
G896MCX	DAF SB3000DKV601	Plaxton Paramount 3500 III	C53F	1989	Ex Shearings, Wigan, 1991
G211VPX	Leyland-DAF 400	Leyland-DAF	B16F	1989	Ex Marchwood, Totton, 1992
G817YPU	Sanos S315.21	FAP Charisma	C53F	1989	
G948VBC	MAN 10-180	Caetano Algarve	C35F	1990	
G348VTA	Volvo B10M-60	Plaxton Paramount 3500 III	C53F	1990	Ex Plymouth Citybus, 1993
H395CJF	Volvo B10M-60	Caetano Algarve	C53F	1990	Ex Anderson Travel, London SE1, 1994
H804EKP	Leyland-DAF 400	Crystals	C16F	1991	
J105BWG	Ford Transit	AVB	M11	1992	Ex Kenning Self Drive, 1994
J722CGT	Leyland-DAF 400	Crystals	C16F	1992	
J864KHD	DAF SB2305DHS585	Plaxton Paramount 3200 III LS	C55F	1992	
K2AME	DAF SB3000DKVF601	Caetano Algarve II	C55F	1993	
K3AME	DAF SB3000DKVF601	Caetano Algarve II	C55F	1993	
K252LGK	Leyland-DAF 400	Leyland-DAF	B16F	1993	
✗ L514EHD	DAF SB2700HS585	Van Hool Alizee HE	C51FT	1994	
L515EHD	DAF SB2700HS585	Van Hool Alizee HE	C51FT	1994	
L951TGT	Leyland-DAF 300	Leyland-DAF	M14	1994	
L952TGT	Leyland-DAF 300	Leyland-DAF	M14	1994	

Livery
White with yellow and two tone blue relief.
Golden Tours fleetnames;- G264EHD, G817YPU, J864KHD, K2AME, K3AME, L514EHD, L515EHD

Cromwell Road in Muswell Hill provides the backdrop for Abbey Travel's ACH972A, a Jonckheere Jubilee P50 on the ubiquitous Volvo B10M chassis. In common with most of the fleet, this vehicle carries the name of an Abbey, in this case Westminster, just visible on the front nearside above the indicator.
Keith Grimes

Originating as the west London arm of Angel Motors, AMR of Bedfont is now a separate company. With the majority of their work centred on Heathrow Airport, Bedfont is an ideal location for the depot where GIL2781 was seen in September 1994. This vehicle features the high-floor version of the Caetano Algarve body mounted on a mid-engined DAF chassis.
Geoff Rixon

Relatively unusual examples of the Mercedes-Benz 0303 are those that carry the Jonckheere Jubilee P50 bodywork style. Anderson's 448DAE is such a coach and is seen in Parliament Square in late September 1994. This type of vehicle was produced in an attempt to encourage operators to purchase the 0303. Colin Lloyd

Typical workhorses of the Angel Motors fleet are the DAF SBs, albeit with a variety of bodywork. Still in the majority are those with Plaxton Paramount bodies, exemplified here by E321EVH crossing Victoria Street in June 1994. Note the array of brackets amidships used to accommodate slipboards when on contract. *Colin Lloyd*

The latest additions to the Angel Motors full size coach fleet are more DAF SBs with the much favoured Van Hool Alizee HE body. Seen here in Hampton Court Way is L514EHD with Golden Tours fleetnames, one of seven similarly adorned examples. *Geoff Rixon*

APPLE COACHES

Apple Coaches Ltd, Stoke Road, Slough, Berkshire, SL2 5AU

GWR980T	Bedford YMT	Plaxton Supreme IV	C53F	1979	Ex Lewis, Llanrhystyd, 1986
PEG632	Ford R1115	Plaxton Paramount 3200	C35F	1984	Ex Hillary, Prudhoe, 1988
B884AJX	DAF SB2300HTD585	Plaxton Paramount 3200	C53F	1985	Ex Smith, Alcester, 1986
F171RAN	Volvo B10M-61	Ikarus Blue Danube 336	C53F	1989	
✗ F172RAN	Volvo B10M-61	Ikarus Blue Danube 336	C53F	1989	
G379MAG	Mercedes-Benz 814D	Coachcraft	C21F	1989	Ex Hardings, Betchworth, 1994

Livery
White with red and green signwriting.

Previous Registration
PEG632   A355OHD

A.& R. INTERNATIONAL

A.& R. International Ltd, Unit F2, Bedfont Industrial Estate, Bedfont Road, Bedfont, Middx

E276MMM	Van Hool T815	Van Hool Acron	C49FT	1988	Ex Spirit of London, Hounslow, 1989
✗ K470PNR	Toyota Coaster HDB30R	Caetano Optimo II	C18F	1992	
K535EHE	Scania K113CRB	Van Hool Alizee HE	C51FT	1993	
K855BUR	Volvo B10M-60	Plaxton Premiere 350	C49FT	1993	
L543XUT	Toyota Coaster HDB30R	Caetano Optimo II	C18F	1994	

Livery
White with red signwriting.
SAS Portman Hotel London fleetnames;- K470PNR

A & R International operate a fleet of five vehicles, among them a pair of Toyota Coasters with Caetano Optimo II bodywork. K470PNR carries a fleetname for the SAS Portman Hotel as it passes the Palace of Westminster on a sunny June day in 1994. Colin Lloyd

ARMCHAIR

Armchair Passenger Transport Company Ltd, Commerce Road, Brentford, Middx, TW8 8LZ

Coach Fleet

JIL3968	Leyland Tiger TRCL10/3ARZM	Plaxton Paramount 3500 III	C53F	1988	
JIL3967	Leyland Tiger TRCTL11/3ARZA	Plaxton Paramount 3500 III	C53F	1989	
JIL3969	Volvo B10M-60	Van Hool Alizee	C49FT	1990	Ex Shearings, Wigan, 1993
JIL3970	Volvo B10M-60	Van Hool Alizee	C49FT	1990	Ex Shearings, Wigan, 1993
JIL3971	Volvo B10M-60	Van Hool Alizee	C49FT	1990	Ex Shearings, Wigan, 1993
JIL3972	Volvo B10M-60	Van Hool Alizee	C49FT	1990	Ex Shearings, Wigan, 1993
JIL3960	Volvo B10M-46	Plaxton Paramount 3200 III	C40F	1990	
JIL3961	Volvo B10M-46	Plaxton Paramount 3200 III	C40F	1990	
JIL3962	Volvo B10M-46	Plaxton Paramount 3200 III	C40F	1990	
JIL3963	Leyland Tiger TRCL10/3ARZM	Plaxton Paramount 3500 III	C50F	1990	
JIL3964	Leyland Tiger TRCL10/3ARZM	Plaxton Paramount 3500 III	C49FT	1990	
JIL3965	Leyland Tiger TRCL10/3ARZM	Plaxton Paramount 3500 III	C50F	1990	
JIL3966	Leyland Tiger TRCL10/3ARZM	Plaxton Paramount 3500 III	C50F	1990	
K321BTM	Volvo B10M-60	Plaxton Premiere 350	C53F	1993	
K322BTM	Volvo B10M-60	Plaxton Premiere 350	C53F	1993	
K323BTM	Volvo B10M-60	Plaxton Premiere 350	C53F	1993	
K290GDT	Volvo B10M-60	Van Hool Alizee HE	C48FT	1993	
K291GDT	Volvo B10M-60	Van Hool Alizee HE	C48FT	1993	
K292GDT	Volvo B10M-60	Van Hool Alizee HE	C48FT	1993	
L116OWF	Volvo B10M-48	Van Hool Alizee HE	C28FT	1994	
L117OWF	Volvo B10M-48	Van Hool Alizee HE	C28FT	1994	
L118OWF	Toyota Coaster HZB50R	Caetano Optimo III	C18F	1994	
L119OWF	Toyota Coaster HZB50R	Caetano Optimo III	C18F	1994	

Previous Registrations

JIL3960	G604XMD, G401XMK	JIL3965	G609XMD, G407XMK	JIL3969	G869RNC
JIL3961	G605XMD, G402XMK	JIL3966	G610XMD, G408XMK	JIL3970	G870RNC
JIL3962	G606XMD, G403XMK	JIL3967	F895SMU	JIL3971	G871RNC
JIL3963	G607XMD, G404XMK	JIL3968	F315RMH	JIL3972	G872RNC
JIL3964	G608XMD, G406XMK				

Livery
Orange and white

ARON COACHES

Aron Coachlines Ltd, 83 Laughton Road, Northolt, Middx, UB5 5LW

C394DML	Bedford YMP	Plaxton Paramount 3200 II	C35F	1985	
F873ONR	TAZ D3200	TAZ Dubrava	C57F	1989	
J466NJU	Dennis Javelin 12SDA1929	Caetano Algarve	C53F	1992	
L21OET	Dennis Javelin 12SDA2131	Plaxton Premiere 320 II	C53F	1994	

Livery
White and orange.

ASHFORD LUXURY

Ashford Luxury Coaches (Middlesex) Ltd, 373 Hatton Road, Bedfont, Middx, TW14 9QS

WWL447T	AEC Reliance 6U2R	Duple Dominant II Express	C53F	1979	Ex Heyfordian, Upper Heyford, 1993
WWL492T	AEC Reliance 6U2R	Duple Dominant II Express	C53F	1979	Ex Heyfordian, Upper Heyford, 1993
OGN879Y	Leyland National 2 NL106TL11/2R	Leyland National	B31D	1983	Ex Capital, West Drayton, 1989
F355DVR	Mercedes-Benz 609D	Mellor	C21F	1989	
F311URU	Dennis Javelin 11SDA1906	Duple 320	C53F	1989	
G855PGA	Ford Transit	Mellor	C16F	1990	
H588CRJ	Mercedes-Benz 709D	Mellor	C21F	1991	
H166EJU	Dennis Javelin 11SDA1906	Duple 320	C53F	1991	
K388PJU	Dennis Javelin 12SDA2117	Plaxton Premiere 320	C53F	1993	
L227BUT	Dennis Javelin 10SDA2139	Plaxton Premiere 320 II	C35F	1994	
M722UWJ	Mercedes-Benz 711D	Mellor	C22F	1994	

Livery
White with two tone blue relief.
WWL447T & WWL492T carry Feltham Aviation fleetnames.

Previous Registrations
WWL447T YPL66T, 9467MU, HIL7403
WWL492T YPL99T, 9682FH

Apple Coaches of Slough operate a small fleet of coaches among which is F172RAN. This low-floor version of the Ikarus Blue Danube body is designated the 336, the more common high-floor version being the 358. It is seen undertaking a private hire excursion to London in July 1994 passing the Houses of Parliament.

Among the four new vehicles taken into stock by Armchair during 1994 is this Van Hool Alizee HE bodied Volvo B10M-48. Not illustrated is the rear badge which professes it to be a Volvo B9. With 28 seats, toilet, and air conditioning (note the pod), L116OWF was being utilised by Japanese tourists in October 1994.

Although Aron Coaches of Northolt are one of the smaller coach operators in the London Area, this does not affect the diversity of the vehicles owned. Depicted here is their TAZ Dubrava F873ONR about to undertake a school contract. Unusually for a small operator, all the Aron Coaches vehicles were purchased new rather than second hand. *Malcolm King*

Including the pair of former Green Line AEC Reliances, all the full size coaches operated by Ashford Luxury are totally British built. Dennis Javelins make up the majority of their large capacity coaches, with K388PJU shown here with bodywork in the shape of the Plaxton Premiere 320 in Bridge Street, Westminster during March 1994. *Colin Lloyd*

AVON COACHES/GATWICK FLYER

G.C. & C.A. Tovey & R.M. Seboa, 90 North Street, Romford, Essex, RM1 1DA
Gatwick Flyer Ltd, 90 North Street, Romford, Essex, RM1 1DA

Avon Coaches fleet

FIL6784	Auwaerter Neoplan N122/3	Auwaerter Skyliner	CH55/20CT	1982	Ex Lattimore, Markyate, 1991
A440JJC	Bedford YNT	Duple Laser	C53F	1983	Ex Young, Romford, 1992
VFJ586	DAF MB200DKFL600	Berkhof Esprite 350	C49FT	1984	Ex Dereham Coachways, 1992
SIB7517	DAF MB200DKFL600	Berkhof Esprite 350	C53F	1984	Ex Chartercoach, Dovercourt, 1992
YSU986	Scania K112CRS	Berkhof Esprite 340	C53F	1985	Ex The Londoners, London SE15, 1993
C708HWC	DAF MB200DKFL600	Berkhof Esprite 340	C53F	1985	Ex London Buses, 1993
C91WCJ	Mercedes-Benz L608D	Reeve Burgess	C19F	1985	Ex Ipswich Travel, 1991
E671DPD	Mercedes-Benz 609D	Crystals	C26F	1988	
F183LVU	Mazda E2200	Made To Measure	M14	1989	Ex Gatwick Flyer, Romford, 1992
K858EWF	DAF 400	Autobus Classique	C16F	1993	

Gatwick Flyer fleet

G236HKY	Citroen C25D	Crystals	M13	1989	
G851LHE	Citroen C25D	Crystals	M15	1990	
J135OBU	Peugeot-Talbot Express	Made To Measure	M15	1992	
K640HNW	Mercedes-Benz 711D	Autobus Classique	C23F	1993	
K650HNW	Mercedes-Benz 711D	Autobus Classique	C23F	1993	

Previous Registrations

FIL6784	SPY375X	VFJ596	A169OHJ
SIB7517	B593XNO	YSU986	B414DHK

Liveries
Avon: White with multicoloured fleetnames.
Gatwick Flyer: White with maroon signwriting.

Gatwick Flyer of Romford operate K640HNW, one of a pair of 23 seat Mercedes-Benz 711Ds with Autobus Classique panel van conversions. It is pictured during a break on the M4 motorway services at Membury during May 1994. Keith Grimes

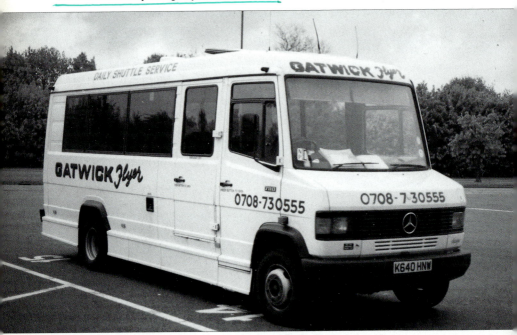

BANSTEAD

Banstead Coaches Ltd, 1 Shrubland Road, Banstead, Surrey, SM7 2ES

✗ MYA525	Bedford OB	Duple Vista	C27F	1950	Ex Five Ways, Croydon, 1985	
TPJ272S	Bedford YMT	Van Hool Mc Ardle 300	C53F	1977		
A212PKK	Peugeot-Talbot Express	Rootes	M12	1984		
D72HRU	Bedford Venturer YNV	Plaxton Paramount 3200 II	C53F	1987		
E466DMY	Freight-Rover 350D	Crystals	C16F	1988	Ex Marksman, Gatwick, 1991	
E232GPH	Bedford Venturer YNV	Plaxton Paramount 3200 III	C55F	1988		
E233GPH	Bedford Venturer YNV	Plaxton Paramount 3200 III	C55F	1988		
F864HGX	Peugeot-Talbot Express	Crystals	M14	1988		
F172XLJ	Dennis Javelin 12SDA1907	Duple 320	C53F	1989		
G951WNR	Dennis Javelin 11SDA1906	Plaxton Paramount 3200 III	C53F	1989		
G952WNR	Dennis Javelin 12SDA1907	Plaxton Paramount 3200 III	C55F	1989		
G433YAY	Dennis Javelin 12SDA1907	Plaxton Paramount 3200 III	C55F	1990		
H722VWU	Scania K93CRB	Plaxton Paramount 3500 III	C53F	1991	Ex Dodsworth, Boroughbridge, 1993	
L164PDT	Dennis Javelin 12SDA2131	Plaxton Premiere 320 II	C53F	1994		

Note: MYA525 is currently undergoing restoration.

Livery
White with pink relief.

BERRYHURST

Domino Finance Ltd, Keltan House, 1 Sail Street, London, SE11 6NG

MUJ208	Volvo B10M-53	Berkhof Emperor 395	CH53/11FT	1985	Ex Kings Ferry, Gillingham, 1992	
✗ MIB644	Scania K112TRS	Berkhof Emperor 395	CH57/19CT	1986	Ex Kings Ferry, Gillingham, 1991	
MIB642	Scania K112TRS	Berkhof Emperor 395	CH57/19CT	1986	Ex Kings Ferry, Gillingham, 1991	
D731BPF	LAG Panoramic	LAG	C24FT	1987		
D654BPL	LAG Panoramic	LAG	C16FT	1987		
E309AGA	DAF SBR3000DKZ570	Plaxton Paramount 4000 II	CH55/19CT	1988	Ex Park's, Hamilton, 1992	
E311AGA	DAF SBR3000DKZ570	Plaxton Paramount 4000 II	CH55/19CT	1988	Ex Park's, Hamilton, 1992	
E657KCX	DAF SB3000DKV601	Van Hool Alizee	C20FT	1988		
E658KCX	DAF SB3000DKV601	Van Hool Alizee	C18FT	1988		
H8BCH	MAN 16.280	Caetano Algarve	C33FT	1991		
J7BCH	Toyota Coaster HDB30R	Caetano Optimo II	C18F	1991		
J9BCH	Toyota Coaster HDB30R	Caetano Optimo II	C21F	1991		

Previous Registrations
MIB642	C691KVW	MIB644	C589KTW	MUJ208	B571AVW

Livery
White and blue or silver and blue.

BEST TOURS

Javaward Ltd, 10 Priory Gardens, London, W5 1DX

D505YPB	DAF SB2300DHS585	Van Rooijen Odysee	C43FT	1986	
✗ F765XNH	LAG Panoramic	LAG	C16FT	1989	
G991FVV	LAG Panoramic	LAG	C16FT	1989	

Livery
Dark metallic blue and white.

Named Vehicles
D505YPB	Globerunner
F765XNH	Globestar
G991FVV	Globehopper

Banstead Coaches are a family owned concern, borne out by the ever immaculate condition of their fleet. Dating from 1977, this Bedford YMT with Van Hool McArdle 300 series bodywork typifies the superb condition of the fleet. The 300 series was Van Hool's first attack on the UK market. TPJ272S was competing at the 1994 Brighton Coach Rally in this view. *Jef Johnson*

Now eight years old and with its second owner, MIB644 is one of the three impressive looking Berkhof Emperors operated by Berryhurst of Lambeth. New to The Kings Ferry as C589KTW, it gained its new registration in 1989 and was acquired by Berryhurst in 1991. It is pictured at its home base in Sail Street near the famous Lambeth Walk. *Colin Lloyd*

Javaward trade as Best Tours, with all three sumptuous constituents of the fleet having names with a global theme such as The Globestar, the name attached to F765XNH. This is one of the LAG Panoramic integral coaches. Seating a mere sixteen passengers, this vehicle's normal use is as a tour bus for pop groups and the like. *Jef Johnson*

BLUEWAYS

Blueways Coaches Ltd, 49 Winders Road, London, SW11 3HE

PIB5268	Mercedes-Benz L608D	Whittaker	C19F	1983	Ex Heptinstall, Allerton Bywater, 1989
PIB5891	Auwaerter Neoplan N116	Auwaerter Cityliner	C34FT	1984	
F634GAK	Mercedes-Benz 811D	Reeve Burgess Beaver	C25F	1989	
NIW5691	DAF SB3000DKSB585	LAG Panoramic	C49FT	1986	Ex Elsey, Gosberton, 1993
K1OLE	Scania K113CRB	Plaxton Excalibur	C36FT	1993	

Named Vehicle
K1OLE   Excalibur

Previous Registrations

NIW5691	C749VDO	PIB5268	A757WHL	PIB5891	A344UFE

Livery
Metallic blue and white or two tone blue with red relief.

Blueways of Battersea operate this rare example of a DAF SB3000 with LAG Panoramic bodywork. Shortly after its launch, LAG decided to only build integral coaches, hence the rarity of the combination pictured. Immaculately turned out for the Epsom Derby is NIW5691. Keith Grimes

Blueways K1OLE was the Plaxton Premiere bodied Scania K113 which appeared at the Coach and Bus Show at the NEC Birmingham in 1991. To date, it remains unique in that no further examples have yet appeared with Scania chassis. Originally used as both a prototype and a demonstrator, it was photographed outside the National Gallery in Trafalgar Square.
David Donati

BOOKHAM COACHES

R.J. O'Reilly & C.A. King, Challacot, Guildford Road, Little Bookham, Surrey, KT23 4HB

MGC337V	Leyland Leopard PSU5C/4R	Plaxton Supreme IV	C50F	1979	Ex Epsom Coaches, 1993
5377RU	Volvo B10M-61	Jonckheere Bermuda	C49FT	1981	Ex NAT, Leeds, 1984
GVS385	Volvo B10M-61	Van Hool Alizee	C57F	1985	Ex Sworder, Walkern, 1989
TSV758	Scania K112CRS	Van Hool Alizee	C53F	1986	Ex BCP Coaches, Gatwick, 1988
TVS986	Volvo B10M-61	Van Hool Alizee H	C53F	1986	Ex Sworder, Walkern, 1989
✗ L7BKM	Scania K113CRB	Van Hool Alizee HE	C49FT	1994	

Previous Registrations
5377RU	WNH142W	GVS385	B238ANK	TSV758	From New
TVS986	D238MKX				

Livery
White with three tone blue relief.

BRENTS / ASTONS

Brents Luxury Limousine & Coach Hire Ltd, Brents House, Imperial Way, Watford, Herts, WD2 4YX

Brents fleet

E647KCX	DAF MB230LB615	Plaxton Paramount 3500 III	C53F	1988	Ex Evans, New Tredegar, 1992
✗ E64SJS	DAF MB230LB615	Plaxton Paramount 3500 III	C51FT	1988	Ex Gordon, Dornoch, 1994
G972KWJ	Mercedes-Benz 811D	Whittaker	C23F	1989	Ex Londoners Tacho, London SE15, 1989
G285STT	Leyland Tiger TRCL10/3ARZM	Plaxton Paramount 3200 III	C53F	1989	Ex Prosser, Bratton Fleming, 1992
G970KJX	DAF MB230LB615	Van Hool Alizee	C51FT	1990	Ex Hallmark, Luton, 1994
G971KJX	DAF MB230LB615	Van Hool Alizee	C51FT	1990	Ex Robinson, Great Harwood, 1994
7804PP	Mercedes-Benz 408D	Whittaker	M12	1990	
H23JMJ	Leyland Tiger TRCL10/3ARZA	Plaxton Paramount 3500 III	C53F	1991	
H24JMJ	Leyland Tiger TRCL10/3ARZA	Plaxton Paramount 3500 III	C49FT	1991	
K337ABH	Mercedes-Benz 814D	Plaxton Beaver	C33F	1992	
K318FYG	Mercedes-Benz 811D	Optare StarRider	C29F	1993	
K712GBE	Mercedes-Benz 410D	Autobus Classique	M12	1993	
K720GBE	Mercedes-Benz 811D	Autobus Classique	C23F	1993	
K108TCP	DAF MB230LTRH615	Van Hool Alizee HE	C51FT	1993	
L513EHD	DAF MB230LTF615	Van Hool Alizee HE	C51FT	1994	
L959JFU	Mercedes-Benz 811D	Autobus Classique	C23F	1994	
L671PWT	Mercedes-Benz 814D	Optare StarRider	C29F	1994	

Astons fleet

✗ YLU910X	Leyland Leopard PSU5C/4R	Duple Dominant III	C57F	1982	Ex Smith, Stanmore, 1994
A991JJU	DAF SB2300DHS585	Plaxton Paramount 3200	C53F	1984	Ex Bennett, Gloucester, 1994
B862XYR	Volvo B10M-61	Plaxton Paramount 3500 II	C51F	1985	Ex Bradley, London E10, 1994
B869XYR	Volvo B10M-61	Plaxton Paramount 3500 II	C51F	1985	Ex Bradley, London E10, 1994
C461JCP	DAF SB2300DHTD585	Plaxton Paramount 3200 II	C53F	1985	Ex Bennett, Gloucester, 1994
C513DND	Volvo B10M-61	Plaxton Paramount 3200 II	C51F	1986	Ex Essex Coachways, London E3, 1994
C518DND	Volvo B10M-61	Plaxton Paramount 3200 II	C53F	1986	Ex Greenhalgh, Ashford, 1994
D542GFH	DAF SB2300DHS585	Plaxton Paramount 3200 III	C53F	1987	Ex Bennett, Gloucester, 1994
G732BVS	Mercedes-Benz 811D	Optare StarRider	C29F	1989	Ex Traject, Halifax, 1992

Previous Registrations
7804PP	G875KKY	YLU910X	OKY823X, CBA1L	D542GFH	D287XCX, PSV111
G732BVS	G686KNW, REP777			

Livery
White with magenta & black fleetnames.

Parked directly opposite the Department of Transport headquarters in Marsham Street is Brents of Watford's E64SJS. It is a DAF MB230 with a Plaxton Paramount 3500 highfloor body. Now eight years old and with its second owner, the condition of the coach does its operator credit.
Colin Lloyd

Astons is a recently formed company owned by Brents of Watford and utilises the same all over white livery with similar style fleetnames. The oldest vehicle in the combined fleets is this Leyland Leopard with trapezoidal-windowed Duple Dominant III style body, seen in October 1994.
Keith Grimes

BRENTONS OF BLACKHEATH

C. Clark, 55-57 Invicta Road, London, SE3 7HD

HVA111N	Leyland Leopard PCU3C/4R	Duple Dominant	C51F	1975	Ex Kenzie, Shepreth, 1980	
SVA924S	Bedford YMT	Plaxton Supreme III	C49DL	1978	Ex Classical, Beeston, 1988	
IDZ2733	Leyland Leopard PSU3E/4R	Plaxton Supreme III	C53F	1978	Ex Cosgrove, Invergowrie, 1981	
IDZ2734	Leyland Leopard PSU3E/4R	Plaxton Supreme III	C53F	1978	Ex Cosgrove, Invergowrie, 1981	
✗ IDZ2735	Leyland Leopard PSU3E/4R	Duple Dominant II	C53F	1978	Ex Wallace Arnold, Leeds, 1984	
IDZ2732	Leyland Leopard PSU3E/4R	Duple Dominant II	C53F	1978	Ex Wallace Arnold, Leeds, 1984	
IDZ2736	Leyland Leopard PSU3E/4R	Plaxton Supreme III	C53F	1978	Ex Bennett, Uxbridge, 1984	
IDZ2737	Leyland Leopard PSU3F/4R	Plaxton Supreme IV	C53F	1980	Ex Wallace Arnold, Leeds, 1986	
A600TGO	Mercedes-Benz L608D	Pilcher	C16FL	1984	Ex Fleet Systems, London, SE18, 1987	
B521WYU	Mercedes-Benz L608D	Reeve Burgess	C19F	1984	Ex Mondial, London, SE13, 1989	
B276AMG	Mercedes-Benz L608D	Plaxton Mini-Supreme	C25F	1985		
C201KGJ	Mercedes-Benz L608D	Plaxton Mini-Supreme	C20F	1986	Ex Epsom Coaches, 1990	
901CDU	Volvo B10M-46	Plaxton Paramount 3200 II	C39F	1987	Ex Bere Regis, Dorchester, 1994	

Previous Registrations

901CDU	From New	IDZ2734	TTS884S	IDZ2736	YPP319S
IDZ2732	XWX185S	IDZ2735	XWX178S	IDZ2737	LUA291V
IDZ2733	TTS883S				

Livery
Cream with red and grey relief.

The latest addition to the Bookham Coaches fleet is this Van Hool Alizee HE bodied Scania K113. Displaying its select DVLC registration L7BKM, it is seen leaving Elizabeth Street, Victoria on 31st August 1994. Colin Lloyd

Brentons of Blackheath operate a fleet consisting mainly of Leyland Leopards and Mercedes-Benz minicoaches. One of a pair of Duple Dominant IIs acquired from Wallace Arnold in 1984, IDZ2735, along with all the Leopards, has been given a Northern Ireland registration plate. Malcolm King

A recent influx of new vehicles has seen eight new Volvo B10Ms with Plaxton Premiere 350 II bodywork enter the Cambridge Coach Services fleet. No. 301 was photographed at London Heathrow coach station a week after entering service. Colin Lloyd

CAMBRIDGE COACH SERVICES

Sovereign Buses Harrow Ltd, Kings Hedges Road, Impington, Cambridge, CB4 4PQ

301	M301BAV	Volvo B10M-62	Plaxton Premiere 350 II	C52F	1994	
302	M302BAV	Volvo B10M-62	Plaxton Premiere 350 II	C52F	1994	
303	M303BAV	Volvo B10M-62	Plaxton Premiere 350 II	C52F	1994	
304	M304BAV	Volvo B10M-62	Plaxton Premiere 350 II	C52F	1994	
305	M305BAV	Volvo B10M-62	Plaxton Premiere 350 II	C52F	1994	
306	M306BAV	Volvo B10M-62	Plaxton Premiere 350 II	C52F	1994	
307	M307BAV	Volvo B10M-62	Plaxton Premiere 350 II	C52F	1994	
308	M308BAV	Volvo B10M-62	Plaxton Premiere 350 II	C52F	1994	
319	G519LWU	Volvo B10M-61	Plaxton Paramount 3500 III	C50F	1990	Ex Wallace Arnold, Leeds, 1994
321	F421DUG	Volvo B10M-60	Plaxton Paramount 3200 III LS	C50F	1989	Ex Wallace Arnold, Leeds, 1993
324	F424DUG	Volvo B10M-60	Plaxton Paramount 3200 III LS	C50F	1989	Ex Wallace Arnold, Leeds, 1992
325	F425DUG	Volvo B10M-60	Plaxton Paramount 3200 III LS	C50F	1989	Ex Wallace Arnold, Leeds, 1992
329	H629UWR	Volvo B10M-60	Plaxton Paramount 3500 III	C50F	1991	Ex Wallace Arnold, Leeds, 1994
350	D350KVE	Volvo B10M-61	Van Hool Alizee H	C53FL	1987	Ex Premier Travel, Cambridge, 1990
351	D351KVE	Volvo B10M-61	Van Hool Alizee H	C53F	1987	Ex Premier Travel, Cambridge, 1990
395	G95RGG	Volvo B10M-60	Plaxton Paramount 3500 III	C53FT	1990	Ex Park's, Hamilton, 1993
396	G96RGG	Volvo B10M-60	Plaxton Paramount 3500 III	C53FT	1990	Ex Park's, Hamilton, 1991
397	G97RGG	Volvo B10M-60	Plaxton Paramount 3500 III	C53FT	1990	Ex Park's, Hamilton, 1991
398	G98RGG	Volvo B10M-60	Plaxton Paramount 3500 III	C53FT	1990	Ex Park's, Hamilton, 1991
492	K392FEG	Toyota Coaster HDB30R	Caetano Optimo II	C18F	1993	

Named Vehicles (All are Cambridge Colleges)
301 Sidney Sussex College
302 Gonville & Caius
303 Pembroke
304 Clare
305 Selwyn
306 Robinson
307 Newnham
308 Magdalene
319 (Not Named)
321 Corpus Christi
324 Trinity
325 Girton
329 Lucy Cavendish
350 St Johns
351 Homerton
395 Churchill
396 Jesus
397 Fitzwilliam
398 Downing
492 St Catherines

Livery
Blue and grey.

CAPITAL

Capital Coaches Ltd, Sipson Road, West Drayton, Middx. UB7 0HN

	Reg	Chassis	Body	Layout	Year	
	PNM698W	Ford R1014	Duple Dominant	B29D	1981	Ex NCP, Gatwick, 1986
	1816MW	Kassbohrer Setra S215HD	Kassbohrer Tornado	C49FT	1983	
	3262MW	Kassbohrer Setra S215HD	Kassbohrer Tornado	C49FT	1983	
	4967MW	Kassbohrer Setra S215HD	Kassbohrer Tornado	C49FT	1983	
	5141MW	Kassbohrer Setra S215HD	Kassbohrer Tornado	C49FT	1983	
H33	OGN880Y	Leyland National 2 NL106TL11/2R	Leyland National	B31D	1983	Ex NCP, Gatwick, 1989
	5304MC	Volvo B10M-61	Plaxton Paramount 3500	C28FT	1984	Ex Marton, West Drayton, 1987
	1335MW	Kassbohrer Setra S215HD	Kassbohrer Tornado	C48DT	1984	
	4019MW	Kassbohrer Setra S215HD	Kassbohrer Tornado	C48DT	1984	
	5948MW	Kassbohrer Setra S215HD	Kassbohrer Tornado	C48DT	1984	
	6764MW	Kassbohrer Setra S215HD	Kassbohrer Tornado	C48DT	1984	
	6963MW	Kassbohrer Setra S215HD	Kassbohrer Tornado	C48DT	1984	
H34	A543WGP	Leyland National 2 NL106TL11/2R	Leyland National	B31D	1984	Ex NCP, Gatwick, 1989
H35	A544WGP	Leyland National 2 NL106TL11/2R	Leyland National	B31D	1984	Ex NCP, Gatwick, 1989
H36	A545WGP	Leyland National 2 NL106TL11/2R	Leyland National	B31D	1984	Ex NCP, Gatwick, 1989
H37	A546WGP	Leyland National 2 NL106TL11/2R	Leyland National	B31D	1984	Ex NCP, Gatwick, 1989
	7639MW	Kassbohrer Setra S215HD	Kassbohrer Tornado	C48DT	1985	
15	C157TLF	Volvo B10M-61	Plaxton Paramount 3200 II	C43F	1985	
	C158TLF	Volvo B10M-61(shortened)	Plaxton Paramount 3200 II	C43F	1985	
	C159TLF	Volvo B10M-61(shortened)	Plaxton Paramount 3200 II	C43F	1985	
	C161TLF	Volvo B10M-61(shortened)	Plaxton Paramount 3200 II	C43F	1985	
	C162TLF	Volvo B10M-61(shortened)	Plaxton Paramount 3200 II	C43F	1985	
	C163TLF	Volvo B10M-61(shortened)	Plaxton Paramount 3200 II	C43F	1985	
	C206TLF	Volvo B10M-61(shortened)	Plaxton Paramount 3200 II	C43F	1985	
	C257TLF	Volvo B10M-46	Plaxton Paramount 3200 II	C35F	1985	
H27	C855EML	Volvo B10M-46	Plaxton Bustler II	B32C	1986	Ex Ralph's, Langley, 1992
H28	C856EML	Volvo B10M-46	Plaxton Bustler II	B32C	1986	Ex Ralph's, Langley, 1989
H29	C857EML	Volvo B10M-46	Plaxton Bustler II	B32C	1986	Ex Ralph's, Langley, 1989
H30	C858EML	Volvo B10M-46	Plaxton Bustler II	B32C	1986	Ex Ralph's, Langley, 1989
H31	C859EML	Volvo B10M-46	Plaxton Bustler II	B32C	1986	Ex Ralph's, Langley, 1989
	C301FML	Volvo B10M-46	Plaxton Bustler II	B33C	1986	Ex Ralph's, Langley, 1993
	C302FML	Volvo B10M-46	Plaxton Bustler II	B33C	1986	Ex Ralph's, Langley, 1993
	C303FML	Volvo B10M-46	Plaxton Bustler II	B33C	1986	Ex Ralph's, Langley, 1993
	C809TLF	Bedford YMPS	Plaxton Paramount 3200 II	C35F	1986	ex Marton, West Drayton, 1991
	D35ALR	Bedford YMPS	Plaxton Paramount 3200 II Exp	C35F	1986	
	D36ALR	Bedford YMPS	Plaxton Paramount 3200 II Exp	C35F	1986	
	D545KMG	Volvo B10M-61	Plaxton Paramount 3200 III	C57F	1987	Ex O'Connor, London W7, 1989
	E140FLD	Bedford YMPS	Plaxton Paramount 3200 II	C35F	1987	Ex Marton, West Drayton, 1991
H1	E211FLD	Scania N112DRB	Van Hool Alizee L	C47F	1987	
H2	E212FLD	Scania N112DRB	Van Hool Alizee L	C47F	1987	
H3	E213FLD	Scania N112DRB	Van Hool Alizee L	C47F	1987	
H4	E214FLD	Scania N112DRB	Van Hool Alizee L	C47F	1987	
H5	E215FLD	Scania N112DRB	Van Hool Alizee L	C47F	1987	
H6	E216FLD	Scania N112DRB	Van Hool Alizee L	C47F	1987	
H7	E217FLD	Scania N112DRB	Van Hool Alizee L	C47F	1987	
H8	E218FLD	Scania N112DRB	Van Hool Alizee L	C47F	1987	
H9	E219FLD	Scania N112DRB	Van Hool Alizee L	C47F	1987	
H10	E220FLD	Scania N112DRB	Van Hool Alizee L	C47F	1987	
H11	E221FLD	Scania N112DRB	Van Hool Alizee L	C47F	1987	
H12	E222FLD	Scania N112DRB	Van Hool Alizee L	DP30D	1987	
H13	E223FLD	Scania N112DRB	Van Hool Alizee L	DP30D	1987	
H14	E224FLD	Scania N112DRB	Van Hool Alizee L	DP30D	1987	
H15	E225FLD	Scania N112DRB	Van Hool Alizee L	DP30D	1987	
H16	E226FLD	Scania N112DRB	Van Hool Alizee L	DP30D	1987	
H17	E227FLD	Scania N112DRB	Van Hool Alizee L	DP30D	1987	
H18	E228FLD	Scania N112DRB	Van Hool Alizee L	DP30D	1987	
H19	E229FLD	Scania N112DRB	Van Hool Alizee L	DP30D	1987	
H20	E230FLD	Scania N112DRB	Van Hool Alizee L	DP30D	1987	
H21	E231FLD	Scania N112DRB	Van Hool Alizee L	DP30D	1987	
H22	E232FLD	Scania N112DRB	Van Hool Alizee L	DP30D	1987	
H23	E233FLD	Scania N112DRB	Van Hool Alizee L	DP30D	1987	
34	E244FLD	Bedford Venturer YNV	Plaxton Paramount 3200 III	C53F	1987	Ex Marton, West Drayton, 1993
	E245FLD	Bedford Venturer YNV	Plaxton Paramount 3200 III	C53F	1987	Ex Marton, West Drayton, 1993
	1068MW	Kassbohrer Setra S215HR	Kassbohrer Rational	C53F	1988	
	3401MW	Kassbohrer Setra S215HR	Kassbohrer Rational	C53F	1988	
	5877MW	Kassbohrer Setra S215HR	Kassbohrer Rational	C53F	1988	
	E22ETN	DAF SB2305DHS585	Duple 340	C53FT	1988	Ex Glynglen, London N12, 1992
	E23ETN	DAF SB2305DHS585	Duple 340	C53FT	1988	Ex Glynglen, London N12, 1992

	Reg	Chassis	Body	Seating	Year	Notes
✗	E24ETN	DAF SB2305DHS585	Duple 340	C53FT	1988	Ex Glynglen, London N12, 1992
	E388FLD	Bedford Venturer YNV	Plaxton Paramount 3200 III	C53F	1988	Ex Marton, West Drayton, 1993
37	E389FLD	Bedford Venturer YNV	Plaxton Paramount 3200 III	C53F	1988	Ex Marton, West Drayton, 1993
	E625FLD	Mercedes-Benz 609D	Reeve Burgess	B16F	1988	
20	E655FLD	Volvo B10M-61	Plaxton Paramount 3200 III	C53F	1988	Ex O'Connor, London W7, 1989
26	E165OMD	Volvo B10M-61	Plaxton Paramount 3200 III	C57F	1988	Ex O'Connor, London W7, 1989
	E322PMD	Volvo B10M-46	Plaxton Derwent II	B31C	1988	Ex Ralph's, Langley, 1993
	E323PMD	Volvo B10M-46	Plaxton Derwent II	B31C	1988	Ex Ralph's, Langley, 1993
	E324PMD	Volvo B10M-46	Plaxton Derwent II	B31C	1988	Ex Ralph's, Langley, 1993
	E325PMD	Volvo B10M-46	Plaxton Derwent II	B31C	1988	Ex Ralph's, Langley, 1993
	F28NLE	Volvo B10M-46	Plaxton Paramount 3200 III	C39F	1988	Ex Marton, West Drayton, 1993
	F29NLE	Volvo B10M-46	Plaxton Paramount 3200 III	C39F	1988	Ex Marton, West Drayton, 1993
	F30NLE	Volvo B10M-46	Plaxton Paramount 3200 III	C39F	1988	Ex Marton, West Drayton, 1993
	F157NLE	Volvo B10M-46	Plaxton Paramount 3200 III	C35F	1988	Ex Marton, West Drayton, 1993
	F544TLU	Mercedes-Benz 811D	Optare StarRider	C25F	1988	Ex KF Cars, Gatwick, 1991
	7572MW	Kassbohrer Setra S210HD	Kassbohrer Optimal	C35F	1989	
	8325MW	Kassbohrer Setra S215HD	Kassbohrer Tornado	C49FT	1989	
	9466MW	Kassbohrer Setra S210HD	Kassbohrer Optimal	C35F	1989	
H32	F134UMD	Mercedes-Benz 709D	Reeve Burgess	C12FL	1989	
	F884SMU	Volvo B10M-60	Plaxton Paramount 3200 III	C57F	1989	Ex O'Connor, London W7, 1989
	G955VBC	Toyota Coaster HB31R	Caetano Optimo	C18F	1989	Ex Happy Days, Woodseaves, 1993
	658COP	Mercedes-Benz 811D	Optare StarRider	C25F	1990	Ex KF Cars, Gatwick, 1991
19	G79BLD	Volvo B10M-60	Plaxton Paramount 3200 III	C53F	1990	Ex KF Cars, Gatwick, 1991
21	G81BLD	Volvo B10M-60	Plaxton Paramount 3200 III	C53F	1990	Ex KF Cars, Gatwick, 1991
22	G82BLD	Volvo B10M-60	Plaxton Paramount 3200 III	C53F	1990	Ex KF Cars, Gatwick, 1991
23	G83BLD	Volvo B10M-60	Plaxton Paramount 3200 III	C53F	1990	Ex KF Cars, Gatwick, 1991
	G144BLD	Volvo B10M-46	Plaxton Paramount 3200 III	C43F	1990	Ex Marton, West Drayton, 1993
	G145BLD	Volvo B10M-46	Plaxton Paramount 3200 III	C43F	1990	Ex Marton, West Drayton, 1993
	G718XLO	Kassbohrer Setra S215HD	Kassbohrer Tornado	C49FT	1990	
	G719XLO	Kassbohrer Setra S215HD	Kassbohrer Tornado	C49FT	1990	
	G720XLO	Kassbohrer Setra S215HR	Kassbohrer Rational	C53F	1990	
	G801XLO	Volvo B10M-60	Plaxton Paramount 3200 III	C53F	1990	
	G802XLO	Volvo B10M-60	Plaxton Paramount 3200 III	C53F	1990	
	G803XLO	Volvo B10M-46	Plaxton Paramount 3200 III	C43F	1990	Ex Marton, West Drayton, 1993
	G804XLO	Volvo B10M-46	Plaxton Paramount 3200 III	C43F	1990	Ex Marton, West Drayton, 1993
	H561FLE	Mercedes-Benz 609D	North West Coach Sales	C16F	1990	Ex KF Cars, Gatwick, 1990
12	H562FLE	Mercedes-Benz 609D	North West Coach Sales	C16F	1990	
	H843UUA	DAF SB220LC550	Optare Delta	B32D	1990	Ex KF Cars, Gatwick, 1991
	1093MW	Kassbohrer Setra S215HR	Kassbohrer Rational	C53F	1991	
	5579MW	Kassbohrer Setra S215HR	Kassbohrer Rational	C35DL	1991	
	9679MW	Kassbohrer Setra S215HR	Kassbohrer Rational	C53F	1991	
	H478FLD	Kassbohrer Setra S210H	Kassbohrer Optimal	C28FT	1991	
	H479FLD	Kassbohrer Setra S210H	Kassbohrer Optimal	C28FT	1991	
	H684FLD	Kassbohrer Setra S215HR	Kassbohrer Rational	C49FT	1991	
	H716FLD	Volvo B10M-46	Plaxton Paramount 3200 III	C43F	1991	Ex Marton, West Drayton, 1993
	H717FLD	Volvo B10M-46	Plaxton Paramount 3200 III	C43F	1991	Ex Marton, West Drayton, 1993
	H837GLD	Mercedes-Benz 609D	North West Coach Sales	C13F	1991	Ex Marton, West Drayton, 1992
	J135LLK	Toyota Coaster HDB30R	Caetano Optimo II	C18F	1991	Ex Marton, West Drayton, 1993
	J136LLK	Toyota Coaster HDB30R	Caetano Optimo II	C18F	1991	Ex Marton, West Drayton, 1993
	J137LLK	Toyota Coaster HDB30R	Caetano Optimo II	C18F	1991	Ex Marton, West Drayton, 1993
	J502LRY	Toyota Coaster HDB30R	Caetano Optimo II	C18F	1991	Ex Marton, West Drayton, 1993
	J503LRY	Toyota Coaster HDB30R	Caetano Optimo II	C18F	1991	
	A5COP	Mercedes-Benz 811D	Optare StarRider	C25F	1992	
	J329LLK	Volvo B10M-46	Plaxton Paramount 3200 III	C43F	1992	Ex Marton, West Drayton, 1993
	J330LLK	Volvo B10M-46	Plaxton Paramount 3200 III	C43F	1992	Ex Marton, West Drayton, 1993
	J331LLK	Volvo B10M-46	Plaxton Paramount 3200 III	C43F	1992	Ex Marton, West Drayton, 1993
	J332LLK	Volvo B10M-46	Plaxton Paramount 3200 III	C43F	1992	Ex Marton, West Drayton, 1993
	J432LLK	Volvo B10M-60	Plaxton Paramount 3200 III	C53F	1992	
17	J433LLK	Volvo B10M-60	Plaxton Paramount 3200 III	C53F	1992	
	K40CAP	Volvo B10M-46	Plaxton Premiere 320	C43F	1993	
	K50CAP	Volvo B10M-46	Plaxton Premiere 320	C43F	1993	
	K60CAP	Volvo B10M-46	Plaxton Premiere 320	C43F	1993	
	K70CAP	Volvo B10M-46	Plaxton Premiere 320	C43F	1993	
	K80CAP	Volvo B10M-46	Plaxton Premiere 320	C43F	1993	
	K90CAP	Volvo B10M-60	Plaxton Premiere 320	C53F	1993	
✗	K100CAP	Volvo B10M-60	Plaxton Premiere 320	C53F	1993	
	K200CAP	Volvo B10M-60	Plaxton Premiere 320	C53F	1993	
	K400CAP	Volvo B10M-60	Plaxton Premiere 320	C53F	1993	
	K500CAP	Volvo B10M-60	Plaxton Premiere 320	C53F	1993	
	K2NCP	Mercedes-Benz 811D	Plaxton Beaver	B23F	1993	
	K3NCP	Mercedes-Benz 811D	Plaxton Beaver	B23F	1993	
	K4NCP	Mercedes-Benz 811D	Plaxton Beaver	B23F	1993	
	K5NCP	Mercedes-Benz 811D	Plaxton Beaver	B23F	1993	

During 1993, Capital took delivery of ten new Plaxton Premiere 320s on Volvo B10M chassis, all with select DVLC registrations. Five of the batch were built on the short length B10M-46 chassis and the remainder, as typified here by K100CAP at Hampton Court, on the more usual B10M-60 type. Geoff Rixon

6	L6NCP	Dennis Dart 9SDL3011	Plaxton Pointer	B25D	1993	
7	L7NCP	Dennis Dart 9SDL3011	Plaxton Pointer	B25D	1993	
8	L8NCP	Dennis Dart 9SDL3011	Plaxton Pointer	B25D	1993	
9	L9NCP	Dennis Dart 9SDL3011	Plaxton Pointer	B25D	1993	
	L204ULX	Mercedes-Benz 709D	Plaxton Beaver	B18FL	1993	
	L205ULX	Mercedes-Benz 709D	Plaxton Beaver	B18FL	1993	
	L206ULX	Mercedes-Benz 709D	Plaxton Beaver	B18FL	1993	
3	L267ULX	Dennis Dart 9SDL3011	Plaxton Pointer	B25D	1993	
2	L268ULX	Dennis Dart 9SDL3011	Plaxton Pointer	B25D	1993	
5	L269ULX	Dennis Dart 9SDL3011	Plaxton Pointer	B25D	1993	
4	L270ULX	Dennis Dart 9SDL3011	Plaxton Pointer	B25D	1993	
X	L30CAP	Volvo B10M-62	Jonckheere Deauville 45L	C28FT	1994	
	L701CNR	Toyota Coaster HZB50R	Caetano Optimo III	C18F	1994	
	L702CNR	Toyota Coaster HZB50R	Caetano Optimo III	C18F	1994	
	L703CNR	Toyota Coaster HZB50R	Caetano Optimo III	C18F	1994	
	L704CNR	Toyota Coaster HZB50R	Caetano Optimo III	C18F	1994	

Previous Registrations

A5COP	From new	4967MW	From New	8325MW	From New	
5304MC	A999GLD	5141MW	From New	9466MW	7572MW	
1068MW	From New	5579MW	From New	9679MW	From New	
1093MW	From New	5877MW	From New	658COP	H842UUA	
1335MW	From New	5948MW	From New	F544TLU	F935AWW, 658COP	
1816MW	5192MW	6764MW	From New	L267ULX	L3NCP	
3262MW	From New	6963MW	From New	L268ULX	L2NCP	
3401MW	From New	7572MW	9466MW	L269ULX	L5NCP	
4019MW	From New	7639MW	From New	L270ULX	L4NCP	

Liveries
Blue and white with red relief.
Silver blue with red and blue: L30CAP
White with red and black relief: G718XLO, G719XLO

Special Liveries
Copthorne Hotel: A5COP.
Forte Hotels (Blue with claret, turquoise & white signwriting): C161TLF
Radison Edwardian Hotel (White with red & grey signwriting): H478FLD
Sheraton Skyline Hotel (Red and grey): C206TLF, C257TLF
British Airports Authority (White with two tone grey & green relief): A545WGP, C302FML, H843UUA.
British Airports Authority (Yellow): H1-11.
Flightpath (White with blue & grey): H12-23, H837GLD.
Hounslow Hoppa (White & green): L204-206ULX.

DAFs and Duple bodies are a rarity in the Capital fleet, but three vehicles share both. E24ETN is a Duple 340 bodied DAF SB2305 seen soaking up the summer sunshine at Hampton Court Green. Geoff Rixon

Parliament Square finds 1068MW, the oldest of eight Kassbohrer Setra Rationals in the Capital fleet, showing tourists the delights of London. Colin Lloyd

During 1993, Jonckheere restyled and expanded the Deauville range. This coincided with the launch of the new Volvo B10M-62. Capital's L30CAP was an early example of both new types, to the extent that it featured in the publicity material for the launch of the Deauville 45L design. Caught at the Epsom Derby, it is luxuriously appointed with 28 seats and also carries a unique livery. Keith Grimes

CANTABRICA COACHES / LEN WRIGHT BAND SERVICES

Cantabrica Coaches Ltd, 146-148 London Road, St Albans, Herts, AL1 1PQ
Len Wright Band Services Ltd, 9 Elton Way, Watford, Herts, WD2 8HH

NPD108L	Leyland National 1151/2R	Leyland National	B46D	1972	Ex Alder Valley South, 1992	
310CCH	Volvo B10M-61	Jonckheere Jubilee P599	C49FT	1987		
450CCH	Volvo B10M-61	Jonckheere Jubilee P599	C49FT	1988		
612CCH	Volvo B10M-61	Jonckheere Jubilee P599	C49FT	1988		
E557KPE	Kassbohrer Setra S215HD	Kassbohrer Tornado	C32FT	1988	Ex Crystal, Radcliffe, 1990	
F958RNV	Volvo B10M-61	Jonckheere Jubilee P599	C32FT	1988		
J100CCH	Volvo B10M-60	Berkhof Excellence 2000 HL	C50FT	1992		
J200CCH	Volvo B10M-60	Berkhof Excellence 2000 HL	C50FT	1992		
J300CCH	Volvo B10M-60	Berkhof Excellence 2000 HL	C50FT	1992		
J400CCH	Volvo B10M-60	Berkhof Excellence 2000 HL	C50FT	1992		
J500CCH	Volvo B10M-60	Berkhof Excellence 2000 HL	C50FT	1992		
K600CCH	Volvo B10M-60	Berkhof Excellence 2000 HL	C50FT	1992		
K700CCH	Volvo B10M-60	Berkhof Excellence 2000 HL	C50FT	1993		
K800CCH	Volvo B10M-60	Berkhof Excellence 2000 HL	C50FT	1993		
K900CCH	Volvo B10M-60	Berkhof Excellence 2000 HL	C50FT	1993		
K999CCH	Volvo B10M-60	Berkhof Excellence 2000 HL	C48FT	1993		
L7CCH	Volvo B10M-62	Berkhof Excellence 2000 HL	C50FT	1994		
L8CCH	Volvo B10M-62	Berkhof Excellence 2000 HL	C50FT	1994		
L9CCH	Volvo B10M-62	Berkhof Excellence 2000 HL	C50FT	1994		
L10CCH	Volvo B10M-62	Berkhof Excellence 2000 HL	C46FT	1994		

Len Wright Band Services Fleet

WSV505	Volvo B10M-61	Van Hool Astral	CH33/13DT	1984	Ex Cantabrica, Watford, 1991
E689NNH	Scania K112CRS	Jonckheere Jubilee P599	C14FT	1988	Ex Cantabrica, Watford, 1991
E690NNH	Scania K112CRS	Jonckheere Jubilee P599	C16FT	1988	Ex Cantabrica, Watford, 1991
F959RNV	Volvo B10M-61	Jonckheere Jubilee P599	C14FT	1988	Ex Cantabrica, Watford, 1991
F68SMC	Volvo B10M-53	Van Hool Astral 3	CH8/0FT	1988	Ex Cantabrica, Watford, 1991
G95VMM	Volvo B10M-50	Van Hool Astral 3	CH21/6FT	1989	Ex Cantabrica, Watford, 1991
G96VMM	Volvo B10M-50	Van Hool Astral 3	CH21/5FT	1989	Ex Cantabrica, Watford, 1991
K2LWB	Scania K113CRB	Plaxton Premiere 350	C14FT	1993	
K2LRT	Volvo B12 (Left hand drive)	Plaxton Prestige	C14FT	1994	

Note: The seating capacity on most of this fleet is variable.

Named Vehicles

F68SMC	Gold II	G95VMM	Gold III	G96VMM	Gold IV

Previous Registrations

310CCH	D31RKX	612CCH	E36EBH	K600CCH	K771XRO
450CCH	E35EBH	WSV505	A59OTA		

Liveries
Cantabrica: Navy blue and red.
Len Wright: Metallic grey and red.

CAVALIER

A.W. Pagan, 87 Fleetside, West Molesey, Surrey, KT8 0NG

D170HML	Mercedes-Benz 609D	Reeve Burgess	C19F	1987	Ex Oakley Coaches, 1993
J461LLK	Sanos S311.21	FAP Charisma	C35FT	1992	Ex Hamilton, Uxbridge, 1993
K706RNR	Toyota Coaster HDB30R	Caetano Optimo II	C21F	1993	
K709RNR	Toyota Coaster HDB30R	Caetano Optimo II	C18F	1993	
L698CNR	Toyota Coaster HZB50R	Caetano Optimo III	C18F	1994	

Livery
White with blue signwriting.

CHALFONT

Chalfont Coaches of Harrow Ltd, 200 Featherstone Road, Southall, Middx, UB2 5AG

WBB330T	Volvo B58-61	Plaxton Supreme IV	C57F	1979	Ex Wansbeck, Ashington, 1985
KPP619V	Ford R1014	Duple Dominant	C35F	1979	
EWE671V	Ford R1114	Duple Dominant II	C53F	1980	
MNT595W	Volvo B58-56	Plaxton Supreme IV Express	C53F	1981	Ex Vagg, Knockin Heath, 1983
RNK324W	Ford R1114	Duple Dominant II	C53F	1981	
SGS510W	Volvo B58-61	Plaxton Viewmaster IV	C36FT	1981	Ex Burrows, Hounslow, 1986
BBY431Y	Ford R1115	Duple Dominant IV	C53F	1982	
E328FLD	Volvo B10M-61	Plaxton Paramount 3200 III	C57F	1987	
E329FLD	Volvo B10M-61	Plaxton Paramount 3200 III	C57F	1987	
F306RMH	Volvo B10M-61	Plaxton Paramount 3500 III	C57F	1987	
F307RMH	Volvo B10M-61	Plaxton Paramount 3500 III	C57F	1987	
F896NWC	Freight-Rover Sherpa	Adams	C16F	1988	Ex Fisher, Deadmans Cross, 1993
H158DJU	Volvo B10M-60	Plaxton Paramount 3200 III	C57F	1990	
H426DVM	Peugeot-Talbot Express	Made to Measure	M12	1990	Ex Fisher, Deadmans Cross, 1993
H487FGL	Volvo B10M-60	Van Hool Alizee H	C49FT	1990	Ex Ford, Gunnislake, 1993
L253LDT	Leyland-DAF 400	Autobus Classique	C16F	1993	
M886SKU	LDV 400	Autobus Classique	C16F	1994	
M860TYC	Volvo B10M-62	Van Hool Alizee HE	C46FT	1994	
M861TYC	Volvo B10M-62	Van Hool Alizee HE	C53FT	1994	
M862TYC	Volvo B10M-62	Van Hool Alizee HE	C57F	1994	

Livery
White and purple.

CHALFONT LINE

T.J. Reynolds, 4 Medway Parade, Perivale, Middx, UB6 8HA

PNB797W	Ford R1114	Plaxton Supreme IV	C49DL	1981	Ex Shearings, Whitchurch, 1986
ABM767X	Ford Transit	Mellor	C14FL	1982	
A202RUR	Mercedes-Benz L307D	Reeve Burgess	M12	1984	Ex City Central, London SE1, 1992
C211FMF	Volvo B10M-61	Plaxton Paramount 3200 II	C51DL	1986	Ex O'Connor, London W7, 1990
E608AWA	Mercedes-Benz L608D	Whittaker	C23FL	1988	Ex Gosling, Redbourn, 1993
G293DOV	Renault Master T35D	Jubilee (1993)	M10	1990	Ex private owner, 1993
H512BND	Mercedes-Benz 609D	Made To Measure	C23FL	1990	Ex Oates, Smallfield, 1991
H271ACK	Fiat Ducato	Jubilee	M11L	1991	
K228TRG	Leyland-DAF 400	Jubilee	M10L	1993	
L531YHA	Leyland-DAF 400	Jubilee Cruisemaster	C16FL	1993	

Livery
White

Named Vehicles
PNB797W	Liberator III	C211FMF	Liberator VI

CHANNEL COACHWAYS

Cherrybriar Ltd, Supreme House, Stour Wharf, Stour Road, Bow, London, E3 2NT

FSK868	Kassbohrer Setra S228DT	Kassbohrer Imperial	CH54/20CT	1986	Ex Channel Coachways, Rochford, 1993
SIB9025	Bedford YMP	Plaxton Paramount 3200 III	C35F	1987	Ex Channel Coachways, Rochford, 1993
SIB6806	Leyland Royal Tiger B50	Van Hool Alizee H	C53F	1987	Ex Boro'line Maidstone, 1993
MIW2416	Iveco 315	Caetano Algarve	C24F	1989	Ex Silvergray Carriage Co, Bedfont, 1993
F790TLW	LAG Panoramic	LAG	C32FT	1989	Ex AML, Hounslow, 1993
G736LEP	DAF 400	Concept	C16F	1990	Ex Channel Coachways, Rochford, 1993
H12CHN	Mercedes-Benz 811D	Optare StarRider	C29F	1991	Ex Channel Coachways, Rochford, 1993
H14CHN	Volvo B10M-60	Ikarus Blue Danube 358	C57F	1991	Ex Channel Coachways, Rochford, 1993
J14CHN	Scania K93CRB	Duple 320	C55FT	1991	Ex Channel Coachways, Rochford, 1993

Previous Registrations
FSK868	C357KGG	SIB9025	D802ALR	H12CHN	H849UUA
MIW2416	F197PNR	F790TLW	F505YNV, A16AML	H14CHN	H301VWJ
SIB6806	D123HMT			J14CHN	J215XKY

Livery
White with blue and red relief.

Since 1992, all new vehicles purchased by Cantabrica have been Volvo B10Ms with the impressive Berkhof Excellence 2000 HL body. J400CCH approaches the usual Sunday afternoon changeover point at Scratchwood Motorway Services in July 1994.
Colin Lloyd

Len Wright Band Services are associated with Cantabrica and, as their fleetname implies, supply the coaching needs of pop groups and bands on tour. As a consequence, the seating on their vehicles is limited, space being more important than seating capacity. This uncommon tri-axled Van Hool Astral 3 seats a mere 23.
Colin Lloyd

Cavalier of West Molesey operate a six vehicle fleet among which are three Toyota Coasters with the inevitable Caetano Optimo body. This view of K706RNR clearly shows the MkII version of the Optimo minicoach, photographed near Hampton Court.
Geoff Rixon

The distinctive white and purple livery afforded to Chalfont's H487FGL is shown to good effect in this shot taken round the corner from Victoria Station in Bressenden Place. It is the oldest of four Van Hool Alizees operated. Colin Lloyd

The newest vehicle in the Chalfont Line fleet is this Jubilee Cruisemaster bodied conversion based on the high roofed Leyland-DAF van. This particular example features sixteen seats with a rear mounted wheelchair lift. L531YHA was seen proceeding along Buckingham Palace Road, Victoria in August 1994. Colin Lloyd

Channel Coachways have long been associated with Rochford in Essex, although they are now based in the East End of London. Here SIB9025, a Bedford YMP with a short Plaxton Paramount body, approaches Tattenham Corner on Derby Day 1994. Colin Lloyd

CHECKER TRAVEL

Checker Cars Ltd, Station Approach, Pinner, Middx, HA5 5LZ

TJH683M	Leyland Leopard PSU3B/4R	Plaxton Panorama Elite III	C53F	1974	Ex Thorpe, London W10, 1991
VCW85V	Leyland Leopard PSU3F/5R	Plaxton Supreme IV	C53F	1979	Ex Thorpe, London W10, 1991
FKK615Y	DAF MB200DKTL600	Plaxton Supreme V	C53F	1983	Ex Paterson, Hamilton, 1994
TSC697Y	Mercedes-Benz L608D	Reeve Burgess	C25F	1983	Ex Crystals, Orpington, 1988
✗ YPD145Y	Leyland Tiger TRCTL11/2R	Duple Dominant IV Express	C53F	1983	Ex BTS, Borehamwood, 1992
SLU261	Ford Transit	Williams Deansgate	M12	1987	Ex Wings, Hayes, 1989
D296RKW	Leyland Tiger TRCTL11/3RZ	Duple 320	C57F	1987	Ex Pan Atlas, London W3, 1993
E428YDM	Mercedes-Benz 609D	PMT Hanbridge	C26F	1987	Ex WLT, Tylers Green, 1990
F576FHA	Ford Transit	Ford	M11	1989	Ex Non PCV, 1992
G40OHS	Ford Transit	Dormobile	B16F	1989	Ex McKenna, Uddingston, 1991
J465UFS	Mercedes-Benz 609D	Crystals	C24F	1992	Ex MacPherson, Roslin, 1994

Previous Registration
SLU261   D969MDB, WET880

Livery
White with black relief.

CHIVERS COACHES

Chivers Coaches Ltd, 173 Stafford Road, Wallington, Surrey, SM6 9BT

✗ DYW168V	Volvo B58-56	Plaxton Supreme IV	C38C	1979	Ex Clarke, London SE20, 1988
NKU962X	Leyland Tiger TRCTL11/3R	Plaxton Supreme IV	C57F	1981	Ex Mosley, Barugh Green, 1985
ESU264	Bedford YMP	Plaxton Paramount 3200	C38F	1984	Ex Armchair, Brentford, 1990
B268TLJ	Bedford YMP	Plaxton Paramount 3200 II	C35F	1985	Ex Athelstan, Malmesbury, 1989
E897XGK	Mercedes-Benz 609D	Reeve Burgess Beaver	C25F	1987	
G836VAY	Toyota Coaster HB31R	Caetano Optimo	C21F	1989	Ex Ross, Wrexham, 1992

Previous Registration
ESU264   A842PPP

Livery
Silver-blue and white.

CLAREMONT

Claremont Coaches Ltd, 246 Longfellow Road, Worcester Park, Surrey, KT4 8AT

RHO711P	Bedford YRQ	Duple Dominant	C45F	1975	Ex Gale, Haslemere, 1979
GPA616V	Volvo B58-56	Plaxton Supreme IV	C53F	1980	Ex Richardson, London SW14, 1984
✗ YGT619W	Volvo B58-56	Plaxton Supreme IV	C53F	1981	Ex Richardson, London SW14, 1985
D570KJT	Volvo B10M-61	Plaxton Paramount 3200 III	C53F	1987	Ex Excelsior, Bournemouth, 1989
D571KJT	Volvo B10M-61	Plaxton Paramount 3200 III	C53F	1987	Ex Excelsior, Bournemouth, 1989
D572KJT	Volvo B10M-61	Plaxton Paramount 3200 III	C53F	1987	Ex Excelsior, Bournemouth, 1989
D613KJT	Volvo B10M-61	Plaxton Paramount 3200 III	C53F	1987	Ex Excelsior, Bournemouth, 1989
F489WPR	Toyota Coaster HB31R	Caetano Optimo	C18F	1989	

Previous Registrations
D570KJT   D268HFX, XEL31   D572KJT   D265HFX, XEL941
D571KJT   D266HFX, XEL158   D613KJT   D269HFX, XEL14

Livery
White and turquoise with ochre relief.

CLARKE'S OF LONDON

E. Clarke & Son (Coaches) Ltd, Kangley Bridge Road, Lower Sydenham, London, SE26 5AT

Reg	Chassis	Body	Type	Year	Notes
BIL1124	Volvo B10M-53	Plaxton Paramount 4000 IIRS	CH55/12CT	1986	Ex Flight, Handsworth, 1990
BIL1816	Volvo B10M-53	Plaxton Paramount 4000 IIRS	CH55/12CT	1986	Ex Flight, Handsworth, 1990
D106BNV	Volvo B10M-61	Jonckheere Jubilee P50	C53F	1987	
D107BNV	Volvo B10M-61	Jonckheere Jubilee P50	C53F	1987	
D108BNV	Volvo B10M-61	Jonckheere Jubilee P50	C53F	1987	
D109BNV	Volvo B10M-61	Jonckheere Jubilee P50	C53F	1987	
D24CNR	Volvo B10M-61	Van Hool Alizee H	C53F	1987	
D25CNR	Volvo B10M-61	Van Hool Alizee H	C53F	1987	
D969RNC	Volvo B10M-61	Plaxton Paramount 3500 III	C53F	1987	
D970RNC	Volvo B10M-61	Plaxton Paramount 3500 III	C53F	1987	
E455SEL	Volvo B10M-61	Van Hool Alizee H	C49FT	1987	Ex Excelsior, Bournemouth, 1992
BIL1878	DAF SBR3000DKZ570	Plaxton Paramount 4000 II	CH55/19CT	1988	Ex Park's, Hamilton, 1992
BIL1977	DAF SBR3000DKZ570	Plaxton Paramount 4000 II	CH55/19CT	1988	Ex Park's, Hamilton, 1992
E426EVS	Volvo B10M-61	Van Hool Alizee H	C53F	1988	
E216JJF	Volvo B10M-61	Van Hool Alizee H	C53F	1988	
E217JJF	Volvo B10M-61	Van Hool Alizee H	C53F	1988	
E218JJF	Volvo B10M-61	Van Hool Alizee H	C53F	1988	
E219JJF	Volvo B10M-61	Van Hool Alizee H	C53F	1988	
E220JJF	Volvo B10M-61	Van Hool Alizee H	C53F	1988	
E221JJF	Volvo B10M-61	Van Hool Alizee H	C53F	1988	
E222LBC	Volvo B10M-61	Van Hool Alizee H	C53F	1988	
E223LBC	Volvo B10M-61	Van Hool Alizee H	C53F	1988	
E301OPR	Volvo B10M-61	Van Hool Alizee H	C49FT	1988	Ex Excelsior, Bournemouth, 1992
E309OPR	Volvo B10M-61	Van Hool Alizee H	C49FT	1988	Ex Excelsior, Bournemouth, 1992
E310OPR	Volvo B10M-61	Van Hool Alizee H	C49FT	1988	Ex Excelsior, Bournemouth, 1992
E311OPR	Volvo B10M-61	Van Hool Alizee H	C49FT	1988	Ex Excelsior, Bournemouth, 1992
F167RJF	Volvo B10M-60	Van Hool Alizee H	C53F	1989	
F168RJF	Volvo B10M-60	Van Hool Alizee H	C53F	1989	
F171RJF	Volvo B10M-60	Van Hool Alizee H	C53F	1989	
F672TFH	Volvo B10M-60	Van Hool Alizee H	C53F	1989	
F673TFH	Volvo B10M-60	Van Hool Alizee H	C53F	1989	
F674TFH	Volvo B10M-60	Van Hool Alizee H	C53F	1989	
J451HDS	Volvo B10M-60	Van Hool Alizee H	C49FT	1992	Ex Park's, Hamilton, 1992
J452HDS	Volvo B10M-60	Van Hool Alizee H	C49FT	1992	Ex Park's, Hamilton, 1992
J453HDS	Volvo B10M-60	Van Hool Alizee H	C49FT	1992	Ex Park's, Hamilton, 1992
J454HDS	Volvo B10M-60	Van Hool Alizee H	C49FT	1992	Ex Park's, Hamilton, 1992
L100CLA	Volvo B10M-62	Van Hool Alizee HE	C49FT	1994	
L200CLA	Volvo B10M-62	Van Hool Alizee HE	C49FT	1994	
L300CLA	Volvo B10M-62	Van Hool Alizee HE	C49FT	1994	
L400CLA	Volvo B10M-62	Van Hool Alizee HE	C49FT	1994	
L500CLA	Volvo B10M-62	Van Hool Alizee HE	C49FT	1994	
L600CLA	Volvo B10M-62	Jonckheere Deauville 45	C53F	1994	
L700CLA	Volvo B10M-62	Jonckheere Deauville 45	C53F	1994	
L800CLA	Volvo B10M-62	Jonckheere Deauville 45	C53F	1994	
L900CLA	Volvo B10M-62	Jonckheere Deauville 45	C53F	1994	

On order for 1995 are an additional ten Volvo B10M/Jonckheere coaches.

Previous Registrations
BIL1124 C720GOP, BIL1214 BIL1878 E315AGA E455SEL GPL-066(Belgium), XEL24
BIL1816 C730GOP BIL1977 E310AGA

Livery
Turquoise and White.
BIL1878/1977 carry 'Globus' fleetnames.
F674TFH & J451HDS carry 'Miki Travel' fleetnames (In Japanese).

Checker Travel YPD145Y was numerically the last of the London Country TD class. This particular coach spent its earlier years on Green Line work from Amersham garage. It was acquired by Checker having passed via London Country North West and BTS of Borehamwood. It was on a private hire when caught at Great Yarmouth coach park.
Siegmund Dereuther

An interesting vehicle in the fleet of Chivers of Wallington is this Plaxton Supreme bodied Volvo B58. DYW168V is fitted with a centre door and was acquired from Clarke's in 1988.
Colin Lloyd

Worcester Park is the home of Claremont's YGT619W, seen here in picturesque East Molesey during October 1994. It is one of a pair of Plaxton Supremes operated, although the majority of the fleet consist of Plaxton Paramounts. Geoff Rixon

Clarke's of London own four double deck Plaxton Paramount 4000s. A brace carry the standard body on DAFs, the other pair the 4000 RS type with the lower deck saloon behind the rear axles on Volvo chassis. DAF BIL1878 carries the Globus Gateway fleetname as it enters Trafalgar Square with a full load of tourists. *Colin Lloyd*

New to the Clarke's fleet in 1994 were nine Volvo B10M-62s, five with Van Hool Alizee HE bodies and four to Jonckheere Deauville 45 specification. L800CLA is one of the latter quartet seen passing the National Gallery in Trafalgar Square soon after delivery. *P.J. Stockwell*

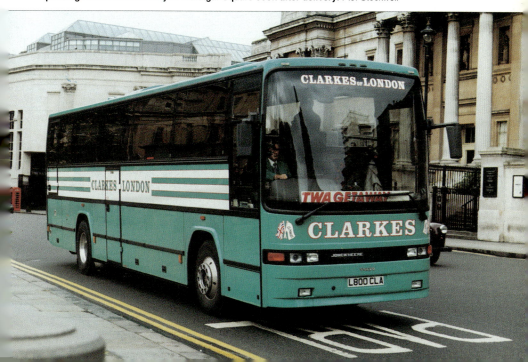

The newest coach in the Collins of Northolt fleet is this low floored example of the integral TAZ Dubrava. It is also the sole coach purchased from new. Epsom Downs is the location on a very hot Derby Day in 1994. Colin Lloyd

COLLINS COACHES

Collins Coaches Ltd, 64 Laughton Road, Northolt, Middx, UB5 5LN

JYJ192N	Volvo B58-61	Plaxton Elite III	C57F	1974	Ex Brown, Crawley, 1994
GUR428N	Volvo B58-61	Plaxton Elite III	C53F	1975	Ex Crocker, St.Austell, 1994
LHE500P	AEC Reliance 6U32R	Plaxton Supreme III	C57F	1976	Ex George, Hare Street, 1983
RLB621R	Volvo B58-61	Plaxton Supreme	C57F	1976	Ex Hawkins, Ruislip, 1983
TGD997R	Volvo B58-56	Plaxton Supreme III	C53F	1977	Ex Negrotti, Greenford, 1984
GSD11R	Volvo B58-56	Duple Dominant II	C53F	1980	Ex Hill, Hersham, 1994
MDS232V	Volvo B58-61	Plaxton Supreme IV	C57F	1980	Ex Ford, Gunnislake, 1987
UUR414W	DAF MB200DKTL600	Plaxton Supreme IV	C57F	1981	Ex Shrubb & Howard, Tatsfield, 1988
NGT2Y	Volvo B10M-61	Plaxton Paramount 3500	C49F	1983	Ex Epsom Coaches, 1990
A511FRM	Volvo B10M-61	Jonckheere Jubilee P90	CH43/9FT	1984	Ex LA Travel, Laindon, 1992
F795TBC	TAZ Dubrava D3200	TAZ	C49FT	1989	

Previous Registrations
A511FRM   A283ERM, 890TT   JYJ192N   VOR555N, VOI8115

Livery
Red, grey and white.

DAVID CORBEL

David Corbel of London Ltd, 6 Camrose Avenue, Edgware, Middx, HA8 6EG

FNK997T	Leyland Leopard PSU3E/4R	Duple Dominant II	C53F	1979	Ex Dunn Line, Nottingham, 1990
BXI477	Van Hool T818	Van Hool Astron	CH49/11FT	1983	Ex Speedbird Coaches, Wembley, 1993
CBA1L	Auwaerter Neoplan N122/3	Auwaerter Skyliner	CH55/20CT	1984	Ex Elite, Stockport, 1993
UJF396	Auwaerter Neoplan N122/3	Auwaerter Skyliner	CH55/20CT	1984	Ex Elite, Stockport, 1993
A8WAY	Sanos S315.21	FAP Charisma	C49FT	1988	Ex Redwing Coaches, London SE5, 1992

Previous Registrations
BXI477   7256DD, RBD41Y   CBA1L   A102MWT, LSV621, A864RUG
UJF396   A106MWT   A8WAY   F60PNO

Livery
Two tone blue and silver.

CUMFILUX COACHES

N.R. Farrow, 69 Corwell Lane, Hillingdon, UB8 3DE

F400CKU	Mercedes-Benz 609D	Whittaker	C24F	1988	
✗ G487KBD	LAG Panoramic	LAG	C49FT	1990	Ex Winstanley & Tomlinson, Tamworth, 1992
L563HNA	Mercedes-Benz 308D	Derwent	C14F	1994	

Livery
White and orange

DAVIAN COACHES

Davian Coaches Ltd, 495 Southbury Road, Enfield, Middx, EN3 4JW

JTM113V	Mercedes-Benz L207D	Reeve Burgess	M12	1979	Ex Franklin, Borehamwood, 1981
XJN202X	Mercedes-Benz L207D	Reeve Burgess	M12	1981	
YJN979X	Mercedes-Benz L207D	Reeve Burgess	M12	1982	
FOO641Y	Mercedes-Benz L207D	Reeve Burgess	M12	1982	
FOO642Y	Mercedes-Benz L207D	Reeve Burgess	M12	1982	
✗ A129MFL	Dennis Dorchester SDA805	Duple Caribbean	C49FT	1984	Ex Young, Rampton, 1986
A61SEV	DAF MB200DKFL600	Berkhof Esprite 350	C57F	1984	Ex Ensign, Purfleet, 1984
✗ C634PSW	MAN MT8.136	GC Smith Whippet	C25F	1986	Ex Armstrong, Castle Douglas, 1987
D29CAC	Scania K112CRS	Plaxton Paramount 3200 II LS	C55F	1986	Ex Oakfield, Enfield, 1994
D41MAG	Iveco Daily 49.10	Robin Hood City Nippy	DP16F	1987	Ex Countybus, Harlow, 1991
E585OEF	Scania K112CRB	Plaxton Paramount 3500 III	C49FT	1988	Ex Aston, Kempsey, 1994

Livery
White with orange and blue.

D & J COACHES

D.Harrington, London City Airport, King George V Dock, Silvertown, London, E16 2PX

Coach Fleet

TMU120Y	Bova EL25/581	Bova Europa	C52F	1983	Ex Dulieu, Dagenham, 1984
✗ G951VBC	Toyota Coaster HB31R	Caetano Optimo	C18F	1989	
H393CJF	Dennis Javelin 12SDA1919	Caetano Algarve	C53F	1990	
L10DJT	Scania K113CRB	Van Hool Alizee HE	C53F	1994	

Livery
White with orange, red and pink stripes with blue fleetnames. (American Express)

EBDON'S TOURS

Ebdon's Coaches Ltd, 1-3 Powerscroft Road, Sidcup, Kent, DA14 5DT

EFW863X	Auwaerter Neoplan N122/3	Auwaerter Skyliner	CH53/18DT	1982
A475HPE	Kassbohrer Setra S228DT	Kassbohrer Imperial	CH54/20CT	1984
E89VWA	Auwaerter Neoplan N122/3,	Auwaerter Skyliner	CH57/20CT	1988
H178RHE	Auwaerter Neoplan N122/3	Auwaerter Skyliner	CH57/22CT	1990
J41XHE	Auwaerter Neoplan N122/3	Auwaerter Skyliner	CH57/22CT	1991
J23XHE	Auwaerter Neoplan N316	Auwaerter Transliner	C49FT	1992
K120OCT	Kassbohrer Setra S215HD	Kassbohrer Tornado	C49FT	1994
L955MWB	Auwaerter Neoplan N116/3	Auwaerter Cityliner	C50FT	1994
✗ M409TWF	Auwaerter Neoplan N117/3	Auwaerter Spaceliner	CH50/6CT	1994

Named vehicles
Ebdon's Cityliner: L955MWB
Ebdon's Imperial: A475HPE
Ebdon's Royale: K120OCT

Ebdon's Skyliner: EFW863X, E89VWA, H178RHE, J41XHE
Ebdon's Spaceliner: M409TWF
Ebdon's Transliner: J23XHE

Previous Registrations

H178RHE	G337KWE	J41XHE	H156RHE

Livery
Claret, white and grey.

Among the many scarce coaches depicted in these pages, David Corbel must rank as having one the most unusual fleets. One such example is this Sanos Charisma which, although it carries the famous triangle on the front grille, is not a Mercedes-Benz. A8WAY is seen parked in Edgware during 1994. P.J. Stockwell

Continuing the trend of uncommon coaches, David Corbel has an integrally built Van Hool Astron T818. Rather than the normal blue and silver shades, this example carries a smart red and white livery as seen in High Street Edgware in October 1994.
Tony Wilson

The sole full-sized coach in the Cumfilux fleet is this LAG Panoramic integral G487KBD. On hire to Ralph's of Langley in August 1994, it is seen rounding Parliament Square with an interested load of Japanese tourists.
Colin Lloyd

Above Unusual vehicles in the Davian fleet are this Dennis Dorchester A129MFL and C634PSW, with relatively uncommon G.C.Smith Whippet design body on the MAN MT8.136 chassis in October 1994.
Keith Grimes

Left Outside the Army & Navy store in Victoria Street stands D & J Coaches G951VBC, a Toyota Coaster minicoach based at the company depot next to the London City Airport in Docklands.
Colin Lloyd

Ebdons Tours of Sidcup are renowned for their use of high specification luxury coaches. Here is F830NNF, a Kassbohrer Setra Tornado with a mere 24 seats but a very high level of internal fitments. As with other Ebdons coaches, it carries a name, in this case Ebdons Royale seen clearly in this shot taken in June 1994 in Cardiff City centre.
Richard Eversden

P & J ELLIS

P.J. Ellis Ltd, 69 Barn Way, Wembley Park, Middx, HA9 9NP

NAG478A	Volvo B10M-61	Jonckheere Jubilee P90	CH49/8FT	1984	Ex SUT, Sheffield, 1987
B494GBD	Volvo B10M-61	Jonckheere Jubilee P50	C51FT	1985	Ex Cantabrica, Watford, 1990
D93BNV	DAF MB230DKFL615	Jonckheere Jubilee P50	C51FT	1987	Ex Lucas, Kingsley, 1990
✗ F960RNV	DAF MB230DKFL615	Jonckheere Jubilee P50	C46FT	1988	Ex Antler, Rugeley, 1990
G981LRP	Volvo B10M-60	Jonckheere Deauville P599	C51FT	1990	Ex Rowley, Emerson Park, 1993
G142MNH	Volvo B10M-60	Jonckheere Deauville P599	C51FT	1990	Ex Ideal Services, Watford, 1993
G143MNH	Volvo B10M-60	Jonckheere Deauville P599	C51FT	1990	Ex Cantabrica, St Albans, 1992

Previous Registration
NAG478A   NNV600Y

Livery
White with red signwriting.

The entire fleet operated by P & J Ellis is made up of Jonckheere bodied coaches, three Deauville P599s, four Jubilees, three P50s and a solitary P90. F960RNV is one of the P50s, seen just having crossed Westminster Bridge in May 1994.
Colin Lloyd

ENFIELDIAN

Oakfield Tours Ltd, Unit 3, 48 London Road, Enfield, Middx, EN2 6EZ

VJD44S	Leyland Leopard PSU3E/4R	Plaxton Supreme III	C53F	1978	Ex Heaney, Enfield, 1991
WRY216X	DAF MB200DKTL600	Plaxton Supreme V	C55F	1982	Ex Wilfreda-Beehive, Adwick-le-Street, 1990
A520NCL	Volvo B10M-61	Plaxton Paramount 3500	C53F	1984	Ex Ralph's, Langley, 1994
F370CHE	Scania K112CRS	Plaxton Paramount 3500 III	C49FT	1988	
✗ G697UNR	TAZ D3500	Taz Dubrava	C49FT	1989	Ex Parkside, Broxbourne, 1990

Livery
White with yellow and blue relief.

EMPRESS OF LONDON

Empress Motors Ltd, 3 Corbridge Crescent, London, E2 9DS

323NAA	Bedford YLQ	Duple Dominant II	C45F	1978	Ex Alpha, Brighton, 1980
AFG985T	Bedford YMT	Duple Dominant II	C53F	1978	Ex Alpha, Brighton, 1980
GIL3129	Bedford YMP	Plaxton Paramount 3200	C35F	1983	Ex Capital, West Drayton, 1990
FSU826	Volvo B10M-61	Plaxton Paramount 3200 II LS	C53F	1985	Ex Excelsior, Bournemouth, 1987
FSU827	Volvo B10M-61	Plaxton Paramount 3200 II LS	C53F	1986	Ex Excelsior, Bournemouth, 1987
FSU828	Volvo B10M-61	Plaxton Paramount 3200 II LS	C53F	1986	Ex Excelsior, Bournemouth, 1987
PJI1830	Volvo B10M-61	Van Hool Alizee	C53F	1987	Ex Farrey, Durham, 1994
LJI8024	Volvo B10M-61	Plaxton Paramount 3200 III LS	C57F	1988	
LJI8023	Volvo B10M-61	Plaxton Paramount 3500 III	C53F	1988	
LJI8022	Volvo B10M-60	Plaxton Paramount 3500 III	C57F	1989	
LJI8025	Volvo B10M-60	Plaxton Paramount 3500 III	C53FT	1989	
LJI3521	Volvo B10M-60	Plaxton Paramount 3200 III	C53F	1989	Ex Excelsior, Bournemouth, 1990
PJI6431	Volvo B10M-60	Plaxton Paramount 3500 III	C53F	1990	Ex Wallace Arnold, Leeds, 1994
PIW2633	Volvo B10M-60	Plaxton Paramount 3500 III	C50F	1990	Ex Wallace Arnold, Leeds, 1994
H572CRJ	Ford Transit	Mellor	C16F	1991	Ex Munro, Uddingston, 1993
PIW2632	Volvo B10M-60	Plaxton Paramount 3500 III	C50F	1991	Ex Wallace Arnold, Leeds, 1994

Previous Registrations

323NAA	AAP2T	LJI3521	F472WFX	PIW2632	H632UWR
FSU826	B915SPR	LJI8022	F717SML	PIW2633	G524LWU
FSU827	C102AFX	LJI8023	F384MUT	PJI1830	D788SGB
FSU828	C103AFX	LJI8024	E166OMD	PJI6431	G552LWU
GIL3129	A93GLD	LJI8025	F718SML		

Livery
Cream with red and black signwriting.

EPSOM COACHES

H.R. Richmond Ltd, Blenheim Road, Longmead, Epsom, Surrey, KT19 9AF

Coach Fleet

PGC339V	Leyland Leopard PSU5C/4R	Plaxton Supreme IV	C50F	1980	
B504CGP	Volvo B10M-61	Plaxton Paramount 3200 II	C53F	1985	
B505CGP	Volvo B10M-61	Plaxton Paramount 3200 II	C53F	1985	
B506CGP	Volvo B10M-61	Plaxton Paramount 3200 II	C53F	1985	
B507CGP	Volvo B10M-61	Plaxton Paramount 3200 II	C53F	1985	
B508CGP	Volvo B10M-61	Plaxton Paramount 3200 II	C53F	1985	
C509HGF	Volvo B10M-61	Plaxton Paramount 3200 II	C53F	1985	
C529DND	Volvo B10M-61	Van Hool Alizee H	C53F	1986	Ex Shearings, Wigan, 1992
C331DND	Volvo B10M-61	Van Hool Alizee H	C53F	1986	Ex Shearings, Wigan, 1992
C510LGH	Volvo B10M-61	Plaxton Paramount 3200 II	C53F	1986	
C511LGH	Volvo B10M-61	Plaxton Paramount 3200 II	C53F	1986	
E512YGC	Volvo B10M-61	Van Hool Alizee H	C49FT	1988	
E513YGC	Volvo B10M-61	Van Hool Alizee H	C49FT	1988	
E514YGC	Volvo B10M-61	Van Hool Alizee H	C49FT	1988	
E515YGC	Volvo B10M-61	Van Hool Alizee H	C49FT	1988	
F516GGJ	Volvo B10M-60	Van Hool Alizee H	C53F	1989	
F517GGJ	Volvo B10M-60	Van Hool Alizee H	C53F	1989	
G518OGP	Volvo B10M-60	Van Hool Alizee H	C53F	1990	
G519OGP	Volvo B10M-60	Van Hool Alizee H	C53F	1990	
H531WGH	Volvo B10M-60	Van Hool Alizee H	C53F	1991	
H532WGH	Volvo B10M-60	Van Hool Alizee H	C53F	1991	
H533WGH	Volvo B10M-60	Van Hool Alizee H	C53F	1991	
J721FGP	Toyota Coaster HDB30R	Caetano Optimo II	C18F	1992	
K460PNR	Toyota Coaster HDB30R	Caetano Optimo II	C18F	1992	
K288GDT	Volvo B10M-60	Van Hool Alizee HE	C49FT	1993	
K289GDT	Volvo B10M-60	Van Hool Alizee HE	C49FT	1993	
K465PNR	Toyota Coaster HDB30R	Caetano Optimo II	C18F	1993	
L231BUT	Dennis Javelin 12SDA2138	Plaxton Premiere 320 II	C53F	1994	
L232BUT	Dennis Javelin 12SDA2138	Plaxton Premiere 320 II	C53F	1994	
L233BUT	Dennis Javelin 12SDA2138	Plaxton Premiere 320 II	C53F	1994	
L234BUT	Dennis Javelin 12SDA2138	Plaxton Premiere 320 II	C53F	1994	

Livery
Cream and maroon with black relief.

Top left **The ever productive Parliament Square provides the setting for Empress of London's AFG985T, one of three different types of Bedfords still in stock. This is the YMT example with the Duple Dominant II body during September 1994. Empress is one of the oldest coach companies in London, dating back four generations to 1923.** Colin Lloyd

Centre left **The majority of the vehicles used by Empress of London are Plaxton Paramount coupled with the erstwhile Volvo B10M. A typical example is LJI3521 about to turn from Millbank onto Lambeth Bridge in October 1994.** Geoff Rixon

Left **Enfieldian is the trading name of Oakfield Tours, although as can be seen, both names are carried. The coaches are garaged at the Paradise Wildlife Park in Broxbourne where G697UNR was parked during November 1994. Of the 50 or so TAZ Dubravas imported into the UK, this coach is one of only a handful that were built to the high floor D3500 specification.** Keith Grimes

Top **The new intake of coaches for Epsom Coaches in 1994 consisted of four Dennis Javelins with Plaxton Premiere 320 bodies. L231BUT heads for Lambeth Bridge.** Geoff Rixon

Above **Private hires account for the majority of the work undertaken by Epsom Coaches. Their Toyota Coaster K460PNR pulls away from Hampton Court Railway Station.** Geoff Rixon

ESCORT COACHES

Mrs H.M. Friedel, 244 Lincoln Road, Enfield, Middx. EN1 1TA

EJP723V	Mercedes-Benz L207D	Devon Conversions	M12	1980	Ex Butcher, Didsbury, 1983
137ASV	Leyland Leopard PSU5C/4R	Plaxton Viewmaster IV	C53F	1980	Ex Spanish Speaking, London NW1, 1986
DLG852X	Mercedes-Benz L207D	Cymric(1985)	M12	1982	Ex private owner, 1992
TSV805	Scania K112CRS	Jonckheere Jubilee P50	C51FT	1984	Ex Cantabrica, Watford, 1990
B154RJU	Mercedes-Benz 0303/15R	Jonckheere Jubilee P50	C51FT	1985	Ex Midland Fox, 1994
B737PLA	Mercedes-Benz L307D	Devon Conversions	M12	1985	
C598TLM	Mercedes-Benz L307D	Devon Conversions	M12	1985	
E241MMM	MCW Metrorider MF150	MCW	C25F	1988	
F176OLB	Fiat Ducato Maxi	Howells	M14	1990	Ex Howells demonstrator, 1991
J123OBU	Mercedes-Benz 609D	Made To Measure	C24F	1991	
K664VNF	Mercedes-Benz 410D	Made To Measure	C16F	1992	

Livery
White with silver, blue and red relief.

Previous Registrations

137ESV	JTM112V		B154RJU	B514CBD, XLC1S
TSV805	A599XRP		K664VNF	J286RNE

On lay-over outside the operating centre in Lincoln Road, Enfield, is Escort Coaches E241MMM during October 1994. It is a Birmingham built MCW Metrorider fitted out to coach specification.
Keith Grimes

ESSEX COACHWAYS / PATHFINDER

Essex Coachways Ltd, Lode Star House, Watts Grove, London, E3 3RE
Pathfinder Luxury Coaches Ltd, 12 Grove Road, Chadwell Heath, Essex, RM6 4AG

Essex Coachways fleet

PNM677W	Ford R1114	Plaxton Supreme IV	C53F	1980	
TMD292Y	Volvo B10M-61	Plaxton Paramount 3200	C32FT	1983	
ADC768A	Volvo B10M-61	Van Hool Alizee H	C53F	1985	Ex Ross, Wrexham, 1994
2588SX	Volvo B10M-60	Van Hool Alizee H	C49FT	1990	
G875RNC	Volvo B10M-60	Van Hool Alizee H	C49FT	1990	Ex Shearings, Wigan, 1992
L970KDT	Volvo B10M-60	Van Hool Alizee HE	C32FT	1993	

Pathfinder Luxury Coaches fleet

D256HFX	Volvo B10M-61	Plaxton Paramount 3500 III	C53F	1987	Ex Excelsior, Bournemouth, 1989
F467MAA	Volvo B10M-61	Van Hool Alizee H	C49FT	1988	Ex Excelsior, Bournemouth, 1992
H92CJU	Volvo B10M-60	Van Hool Alizee H	C51FT	1990	Ex Houghton, Wootten, 1994
J307KFP	Toyota Coaster HDB30R	Caetano Optimo II	C21F	1991	

Previous Registrations
2588SX From new   F467MAA   AYU776 (Belgium), F451WFX, XEL606

Liveries
Essex Coachways: Mustard with white and black relief.
Pathfinder: White with orange and yellow relief.

FALCON TRAVEL

A.J. Risby & R.E. Baldwin, Unit 4, 123 Nutty Lane, Shepperton, Surrey, TW17 0RQ

KBH846V	Leyland Leopard PSU3E/4R	Plaxton Supreme IV	C53F	1980	Ex Frames Rickards, Brentford, 1986
FSK866	Kassbohrer Setra S215H	Kassbohrer Optimal	C53F	1982	Ex York, Cogenhoe, 1989
FSK867	Kassbohrer Setra S215H	Kassbohrer Optimal	C53F	1982	Ex Athelstan, Chippenham, 1990
X RBD72Y	MAN SR280	MAN	C53F	1982	Ex York, Cogenhoe, 1992.
TSU606	Kassbohrer Setra S215HD	Kassbohrer Tornado	C48FT	1985	Ex Birds, North Hykeham, 1994.

Previous Registrations

FSK866	ENH89X, KPR698, GVV128X	TSU606	6097EL, C356JHE
FSK867	VWX360X, 168WAL, YNA484X	RBD72Y	RAM73Y, TVY659

Livery
White with burgundy and black relief.

FINCHLEY COACHES / SOUTHGATE COACHES

Finchley & Southgate Coaches Ltd, 52 Brunswick Park Road, New Southgate, London, N12 1HA

	SHT104S	Ford R1114	Duple Dominant II	C53F	1978	Ex Turner, Bristol, 1985
S	SYU738S	Ford R1114	Duple Dominant II	C53F	1978	Ex Grey-Green, London N16, 1984
S	BRO483T	Ford R1114	Duple Dominant II	C53F	1978	Ex Essex Coachways, London, E3, 1982
S	CVS957T	Ford R1114	Duple Dominant II Express	C53F	1979	Ex Richmond, Barley, 1987
	VHU204T	Ford R1114	Duple Dominant II Express	C53F	1979	Ex Southgate Coaches, London, N12
	BTX36V	Ford R1114	Plaxton Supreme IV	C53F	1979	Ex Cleverly, Cwmbran, 1982
	BTX37V	Ford R1114	Plaxton Supreme IV	C53F	1979	Ex Bailey, Hucknall, 1987
S	BTX38V	Ford R1114	Plaxton Supreme IV	C53F	1979	Ex Cleverly, Cwmbran, 1982
S	BTX40V	Ford R1114	Plaxton Supreme IV	C53F	1979	Ex Rayleigh, Ramsden Heath, 1987
X	KHB30W	Ford R1114	Plaxton Supreme IV Express	C53F	1981	Ex Read, South Woodham, 1987
	NDG585W	Ford R1114	Duple Dominant II	C53F	1980	Ex Perrett, Shipton Oliffe, 1985
S	OHA517W	Ford R1114	Duple Dominant II	C53F	1980	Ex Heart of England, Water Orton, 1987
S	OHP8W	Ford R1114	Plaxton Supreme IV	C53F	1980	Ex Shaw, Bedworth, 1985
	JSV454	Leyland Tiger TRCTL11/3R	Plaxton Paramount 3500	C55F	1983	Ex Armchair, Brentford, 1988
S	UTN455Y	Leyland Tiger TRCTL11/3R	Plaxton Paramount 3500	C51F	1983	Ex Skew, New Milton, 1988
	BYJ575Y	Leyland Tiger TRCTL11/3R	Plaxton Paramount 3500	C53F	1983	Ex Plumpton Coaches, Plumpton Green, 1989
X	A213DPB	Leyland Tiger TRCTL11/3RH	Plaxton Paramount 3200 Exp	C51F	1983	Ex Wycombe Bus Co. 1994
X	A802XEP	Leyland Tiger TRCTL11/3R	LAG Galaxy	C53F	1984	Ex Davies, Pencader, 1989
S	B275AMG	Leyland Tiger TRCTL11/3R	Plaxton Paramount 3200	C53F	1985	Ex Finchley Coaches, London, N12, 1989
	D146HML	Leyland Tiger TRCTL11/3RZ	Duple 320	C53F	1987	Ex Pan Atlas, London, W3, 1988

S - Denotes vehicles licensed to Southgate Coaches.

Previous Registrations

JSV454	FNM864Y	BYJ575Y	YFG391Y, WSV504	

Livery
Yellow with orange and blue relief. Some vehicles carry the previous livery of white with blue relief.

FOREST COACHES

Questcliffe Ltd, The Coach House, Nelson Street, East Ham, London, E6 2QA

EGS174T	Bedford YMT	Plaxton Supreme IV	C53F	1979	Ex Springfield, Wigan, 1993
WCO736V	Volvo B58-61	Caetano Alpha	C53F	1980	Ex Heards, Hartland, 1986
FHS768X	Volvo B58-56	Duple Dominant IV	C46FT	1982	Ex Pettigrew, Mauchline, 1987
WSV532	Volvo B10M-61	Padane ZX	C49FT	1982	Ex Arena, Speke, 1990
DFP974Y	Mercedes-Benz 0303	Jonckheere Bermuda	C49FT	1983	Ex Hookways, Meath, 1992
C519KFL	Leyland Royal Tiger RTC	Leyland Doyen	C53F	1985	Ex Premier, Cambridge, 1989
D209VVV	Iveco 79.14	Caetano Viana	C19F	1986	Ex Angel Motors, London N15, 1994
D760TTA	Hestair Duple 425 SDA1512	Duple 425	C55F	1987	Ex Snells, Newton Abbot, 1993
X E60MMM	Bedford VAS5	Plaxton Paramount 3200 II	C29F	1987	
E249UHL	Freight-Rover Sherpa 350D	Coachcraft	C16F	1987	
G402VML	Toyota Coaster HB31R	Caetano Optimo	C21F	1990	
H406CJF	Toyota Coaster HB31R	Caetano Optimo	C21F	1990	

Previous Registrations   **Livery**
WSV532   ADV142Y   DFP974Y   BDV872Y, 2603HP   White with two tone green relief.

The familiar combination of Volvo B10M and Van Hool Alizee is without doubt the standard choice in the Essex Coachways and Pathfinder Luxury Coaches fleet. L970KDT so far remains unique as the only example with the later Alizee HE body featuring revised grille and headlights as well as structural differences to provide better passenger protection. *Keith Grimes*

As with many foreign coaches, the MAN 280 design was initially imported during the boom years of coaching when most operators were keen to have something a little bit different. Falcon Travel have RBD72Y, one of the slightly more common low-floor version of this design, parked in their Shepperton premises in late 1994. *Malcolm King*

Finchley & Southgate Coaches are two fleets which share the same livery. Depicted in Parliament Square in June 1994, KHB30W is a Ford R1114 with Plaxton Supreme showing the owner's name within its Bristol front dome. Although not obvious, it is in fact one of the Finchley Coaches fleet.
Colin Lloyd

With one exception, the combined operations of Finchley & Southgate can boast totally British built coaches. The odd one is this LAG Galaxy body, on a British Leyland Tiger. A802XEP undertakes one of its more usual tasks of collecting local school children in autumn 1994.
Capital Transport

Forest's E60MMM was one of the very last Bedford VASs to be built. It is also unusual in having a Plaxton Paramount 3200 body. June 1994 finds it at Stratford Bus Station undertaking a works contract. *Colin Lloyd*

FRAMES RICKARDS

Frames Rickards Ltd, 11 Herbrand Street, London, WC1N 1EX

F422DUG	Volvo B10M-60	Plaxton Paramount 3200 III LS	C50F	1989	Ex Wallace Arnold, Leeds, 1993
F423DUG	Volvo B10M-60	Plaxton Paramount 3200 III LS	C50F	1989	Ex Wallace Arnold, Leeds, 1993
F433DUG	Volvo B10M-60	Plaxton Paramount 3200 III LS	C50F	1989	Ex Wallace Arnold, Leeds, 1993
F894SMU	Volvo B10M-60	Plaxton Paramount 3200 III	C53F	1989	
G647WMG	Volvo B10M-60	Plaxton Paramount 3200 III	C53F	1990	
G648WMG	Volvo B10M-60	Plaxton Paramount 3200 III	C53F	1990	
G649WMG	Volvo B10M-60	Plaxton Paramount 3200 III	C53F	1990	
H922DRJ	Scania K93CRB	Plaxton Paramount 3200 III LS	C53F	1991	Ex Shearings, Wigan, 1994
H925DRJ	Scania K93CRB	Plaxton Paramount 3200 III LS	C53F	1991	Ex Shearings, Wigan, 1994
H524DVM	Scania K93CRB	Plaxton Paramount 3200 III LS	C53F	1991	Ex Shearings, Wigan, 1994
H528DVM	Scania K93CRB	Plaxton Paramount 3200 III LS	C53F	1991	Ex Shearings, Wigan, 1994

Livery
Maroon with gold signwriting.

Special Liveries
British Airways Holidays (Blue and grey with red relief): G648 WMG, G649WMG.

GAYTIME

D.J. & I.M.Lock, 48 Vera Road, London, SW6 6QW

	TSV760	Scania K112CRS	Van Hool Alizee H	C49FT	1986	Ex BCP Coaches, Gatwick, 1988
✗	F389RML	Van Hool T815	Van Hool Alicron	C53F	1989	
	M255JBC	Toyota Coaster HZB50R	Caetano Optimo III	C21F	1994	

Previous Registration
TSV760   C242THC

Livery
Grey and silver with white and blue relief.

GOLDENSTAND

Goldenstand Coaches Ltd, 15 Chase Road, North Acton, London, NW10 6PT

	55HLL	Bedford YMT	Duple Dominant II	C53F	1979	Ex Smith, Alcester, 1982
	CAX16X	Ford R1114	Plaxton Supreme IV	C14FTL	1980	Ex Scott, London SE5,, 1986
	IIL9408	Scania K112CRS	Jonckheere Jubilee P599	C57F	1984	Ex Randall, London NW10, 1985
	A71JOY	Iveco 35F8	Robin Hood	M12	1984	
	A72JOY	Iveco 35F8	Robin Hood	M12	1984	Ex Non PSV, 1986
	A75JOY	Iveco 35F8	Robin Hood	M12	1984	
	CIL8589	DAF SB2300DHS585	Plaxton Paramount 3200	C53F	1984	
	A889PPX	Volkswagen LT28	Devon Conversions	M12	1984	Ex private owner, 1992
✗	IIL6265	Scania K112CRS	Jonckheere Jubilee P50	C51FT	1984	Ex Cantabrica, Watford, 1989
	IIL6906	Scania K112CRS	Jonckheere Jubilee P50	C53F	1984	Ex Crawford, Neilston, 1989
	B876EOM	Ford Transit	Robin Hood	M12	1985	Ex private owner, 1986
	C984YFA	DAF MB200DKFL600	Duple Caribbean 2	C53F	1985	Ex Staffordian, Stafford, 1994
	C524TJF	Ford Transit	Rootes	B16F	1986	Ex Fisher, Deadmans Cross, 1992
	K354CRD	Leyland-DAF 400	Pearl	C16F	1993	
	L453FTF	Leyland-DAF 400	Pearl	C16F	1993	
	L403GMO	Leyland-DAF 400	Pearl	C16F	1993	
	M854NCF	LDV Hi Loader	LDV	DP16F	1994	
	M721XOT	LDV Hi Loader	LDV	DP16F	1994	

Previous Registrations

55HLL	BGY605T	IIL6345	A598XRP ✗	IIL9408		A63JLW
CIL8589	A229LFX	IIL6906	B511GBD	C984YFA		C759UVT, MIB581

Livery
White with red relief and black signwriting.

A. GREEN'S OF LONDON

A. Green (Coaches) Ltd, 357a Hoe Street, Walthamstow, London, E17 9AP

	VBH96S	Bedford YMT	Duple Dominant II	C53F	1977	Ex Premier, Watford, 1985
	LSF575X	Volvo B10M-61	Duple Super Goldliner IV	C48FT	1982	Ex Embling, Guyhirn, 1988
	MCN237X	Volvo B10M-61	Caetano Alpha	C53F	1982	Ex Brightman, London NW7, 1989
	THR752	Volvo B10M-61	Plaxton Paramount 3500	C53F	1984	Ex Ralph's, Langley, 1992
✗	G956VBC	DAF SB2305DHS585	Caetano Algarve	C49FT	1990	
	G957VBC	DAF SB2305DHS585	Caetano Algarve	C53F	1990	

Previous Registration
THR752   A700XMH

Livery
White.

Although Volvos make up the majority of the Frames Rickards fleet, the latest additions to the assembly are a quartet of Scania K93s. Acquired from Shearings in 1994, H925DRJ shows the optional low driving position and is seen at Southsea during D-Day commemorations in June 1994. Note the 'By Royal Appointment' coat of arms above the rear wheel. *T.K. Brookes*

Of the eleven coaches operated by Frames Rickards, two are painted in British Airways Holidays livery. G649WMG is such an example awaiting the return of passengers at Hampton Court Station on a bright and dry November day. *Geoff Rixon*

Gaytime of Fulham operate three coaches which alas can prove to be very camera shy! Emerging from the shadows of Putney Bridge is F389RML, an integral Van Hool Alicron. As can be deduced by the sticker in the windscreen, it is powered by the MAN 330 horsepower engine.
Colin Lloyd

Enjoying a day out in Great Yarmouth is Goldenstand A598XRP. One of three Jonckheere Jubilees mounted on the Scania K112 chassis, this vehicle has recently been re-registered IIL6265.
Siegmund Dereuther

A. Green of Walthamstow bought a pair of these Caetano Algarve bodied DAFs in 1990, G956VBC pictured here having 49 seats plus toilet. December 1994 finds the coach rounding Parliament Square on a usual private hire.
Colin Lloyd

GREEN LINE

		a Sovereign	b Bee Line (Q Drive)	c Countybus	d Luton & District		e Guildford & West Surrey
d	192	GIL6253	Volvo B10M-61	Plaxton Paramount 3500 III	C51F	1987	Ex Moordale, Newcastle, 1994
d	193	GIL6949	Volvo B10M-61	Plaxton Paramount 3500 III	C51F	1987	Ex Moordale, Newcastle, 1994
d	137	GIL8487	Dennis Javelin 11SDL1905	Duple 320	C53F	1988	Ex Rochester & Marshall, 1994
d	138	GIL8488	Dennis Javelin 11SDL1905	Duple 320	C53F	1988	Ex Rochester & Marshall, 1994
d	194	HIL7594	Volvo B10M-61	Plaxton Paramount 3500 III	C53F	1987	Ex Moordale, Newcastle, 1994
d	195	HIL7595	Volvo B10M-61	Plaxton Paramount 3500 III	C53F	1987	Ex Moordale, Newcastle, 1994
d	134	HIL7596	Dennis Javelin 11SDL1905	Duple 320	C53F	1988	Ex Rochester & Marshall, 1994
d	196	HIL7597	Volvo B10M-61	Plaxton Paramount 3500 III	C53F	1987	Ex Moordale, Newcastle, 1994
d	135	IIL4579	Dennis Javelin 11SDL1905	Duple 320	C53F	1988	Ex Rochester & Marshall, 1994
d	136	IIL4580	Dennis Javelin 11SDL1905	Duple 320	C53F	1988	Ex Rochester & Marshall, 1994
c	TPL510	OIB3510	Leyland Tiger TRCTL11/3RH	Plaxton Paramount 3200	C53F	1983	Ex Keighley & District, 1992
c	TP70	OIB3520	Leyland Tiger TRCTL11/2R	Plaxton Paramount 3200 II	C49F	1985	
c	TP71	OIB3521	Leyland Tiger TRCTL11/2R	Plaxton Paramount 3200 II	C49F	1985	
c	TP72	OIB3522	Leyland Tiger TRCTL11/2R	Plaxton Paramount 3200 II	C49F	1985	
c	TP75	OIB3523	Leyland Tiger TRCTL11/2R	Plaxton Paramount 3200 II	C49F	1985	
e	376	GOL403N	Leyland National 11351/1R	East Lancs Greenway(1994)	DP49F	1975	Ex Northumbria, 1994
e	373	JOX490P	Leyland National 11351/1R	East Lancs Greenway(1994)	DP49F	1976	Ex Midland Fox, 1994
e	374	UHG744R	Leyland National 11351A/1R	East Lancs Greenway(1994)	DP49F	1976	Ex Midland Fox, 1994
e	375	UFG54S	Leyland National 11351A/2R	East Lancs Greenway(1994)	DP49F	1977	Ex London & Country, 1994
e	377	TPE161S	Leyland National 11351A/1R	East Lancs Greenway(1994)	DP49F	1978	Ex London & Country, 1994
b	719	GGM75W	Leyland Leopard PSU3F/4R	Plaxton Supreme IV	C51F	1981	
d	191	SMY630X	Leyland Tiger TRCTL11/3R	Plaxton Supreme V	C53F	1982	
b	724	SMY631X	Leyland Tiger TRCTL11/3R	Plaxton Supreme V	C53F	1982	Ex Luton & District, 1993
b	726	SMY632X	Leyland Tiger TRCTL11/3R	Plaxton Supreme V	C53F	1982	Ex Luton & District, 1993
d	NTL5	SMY633X	Leyland Tiger TRCTL11/3R	Plaxton Supreme V	C53F	1982	
b	727	SMY637X	Leyland Tiger TRCTL11/3R	Plaxton Supreme V	C53F	1982	Ex Luton & District, 1993
b	752	YPJ203Y	Leyland Tiger TRCTL11/3R	Plaxton Paramount 3500	C50F	1983	Ex Thames Valley & Aldershot, 1986
b	754	YPJ206Y	Leyland Tiger TRCTL11/3R	Plaxton Paramount 3500	C50F	1983	Ex Alder Valley, 1992
b	761	A211DPB	Leyland Tiger TRCTL11/3RH	Plaxton Paramount 3200	C51F	1983	Ex Thames Valley & Aldershot, 1986
b	762	A212DPB	Leyland Tiger TRCTL11/3RH	Plaxton Paramount 3200	C51F	1983	Ex Thames Valley & Aldershot, 1986
b	765	A215DPB	Leyland Tiger TRCTL11/3RH	Plaxton Paramount 3200	C51F	1983	Ex Thames Valley & Aldershot, 1986
d	TP1	A101EPA	Leyland Tiger TRCTL11/2R	Plaxton Paramount 3200	C53F	1983	
d	129	A102EPA	Leyland Tiger TRCTL11/2R	Plaxton Paramount 3200	C53F	1983	Ex LCNW, 1991
b	728	A109EPA	Leyland Tiger TRCTL11/2R	Plaxton Paramount 3200	C51F	1983	Ex Luton & District, 1993
d	TP13	A113EPA	Leyland Tiger TRCTL11/2R	Plaxton Paramount 3200	C53F	1983	
d	TP15	A115EPA	Leyland Tiger TRCTL11/2R	Plaxton Paramount 3200	C53F	1983	
d	TP36	A136EPA	Leyland Tiger TRCTL11/3R	Plaxton Paramount 3200	C53F	1984	
d	133	A145EPA	Leyland Tiger TRCTL11/3R	Plaxton Paramount 3200	C51F	1984	Ex LCNW, 1991
d	TPL50	A150EPA	Leyland Tiger TRCTL11/3R	Plaxton Paramount 3200	C51F	1984	
d	TPL51	A151EPA	Leyland Tiger TRCTL11/3R	Plaxton Paramount 3200	C57F	1984	
d	TPL52	A152EPA	Leyland Tiger TRCTL11/3R	Plaxton Paramount 3200	C57F	1984	
d	TPL53	A153EPA	Leyland Tiger TRCTL11/3R	Plaxton Paramount 3200	C57F	1984	
d	TPL55	A155EPA	Leyland Tiger TRCTL11/3R	Plaxton Paramount 3200	C57F	1984	
d	TPL57	A157EPA	Leyland Tiger TRCTL11/3R	Plaxton Paramount 3200	C57F	1984	
c	TP61	B261KPF	Leyland Tiger TRCTL11/2R	Plaxton Paramount 3200 II	C49F	1985	Ex Sovereign, 1990
d	116	B269KPF	Leyland Tiger TRCTL11/2R	Plaxton Paramount 3200 II	C49F	1985	Ex Sovereign, 1990
d	115	B282KPF	Leyland Tiger TRCTL11/2R	Plaxton Paramount 3200 II	C53F	1985	Ex Sovereign, 1990
d	TPL84	B284KPF	Leyland Tiger TRCTL11/3R	Plaxton Paramount 3200 II	C53F	1985	
d	132	B291KPF	Leyland Tiger TRCTL11/3R	Plaxton Paramount 3200 II	C51F	1984	Ex LCNW, 1991
d	TPL92	B292KPF	Leyland Tiger TRCTL11/3R	Plaxton Paramount 3200 II	C51F	1985	
d	TPL93	B293KPF	Leyland Tiger TRCTL11/3R	Plaxton Paramount 3200 II	C51F	1985	
b	766	B294KPF	Leyland Tiger TRCTL11/3R	Plaxton Paramount 3200 II	C51F	1985	Ex Luton & District, 1993
b	767	B295KPF	Leyland Tiger TRCTL11/3R	Plaxton Paramount 3200 II	C51F	1985	Ex Luton & District, 1993
d	BTL47	C147SPB	Leyland Tiger TRCTL11/3RH	Berkhof Everest 370	C53F	1986	
d	BTL48	C148SPB	Leyland Tiger TRCTL11/3RH	Berkhof Everest 370	C53F	1986	
d	BTL49	C149SPB	Leyland Tiger TRCTL11/3RH	Berkhof Everest 370	C53F	1986	
d	117	C247SPC	Leyland Tiger TRCTL11/3RH	Duple 320	C53F	1986	Ex Sovereign, 1990
d	118	C248SPC	Leyland Tiger TRCTL11/3RH	Duple 320	C53F	1986	Ex Sovereign, 1990
d	120	C250SPC	Leyland Tiger TRCTL11/3RH	Duple 320	C53F	1986	Ex Sovereign, 1990
d	122	C252SPC	Leyland Tiger TRCTL11/3RH	Duple 320	C53F	1986	Ex Sovereign, 1990
c	TDL53	C253SPC	Leyland Tiger TRCTL11/3RH	Duple 320	C53F	1986	Ex London & Country, 1993
c	TDL54	C254SPC	Leyland Tiger TRCTL11/3RH	Duple 320	C53F	1986	Ex London & Country, 1993
c	TDL55	C255SPC	Leyland Tiger TRCTL11/3RH	Duple 320	C49F	1986	Ex London & Country, 1993
b	769	C258SPC	Leyland Tiger TRCTL11/3RH	Duple 320	C53F	1986	Ex Luton & District, 1993
c	TDL60	C260SPC	Leyland Tiger TRCTL11/3R	Duple 320	C49F	1986	Ex London & Country, 1993
c	TDL63	C263SPC	Leyland Tiger TRCTL11/3R	Duple 320	C53F	1986	Ex London & Country, 1993
c	TDL65	C265SPC	Leyland Tiger TRCTL11/3R	Duple 320	C53F	1986	
d	111	E661AWJ	Leyland Tiger TRCTL11/3RZ	Plaxton Paramount 3200 III	C53F	1988	

d 112	E662AWJ	Leyland Tiger TRCTL11/3RZ	Plaxton Paramount 3200 III	C53F	1988	
d 113	E663AWJ	Leyland Tiger TRCTL11/3RZ	Plaxton Paramount 3200 III	C53F	1988	
a 359	E359NEG	Volvo B10M-61	Plaxton Paramount 3200 III	C53F	1988	
b 768	E322OMG	Leyland Tiger TRCTL11/3R	Plaxton Paramount 3200 III	C53F	1988	Ex Luton & District, 1993
d TPL98	E323OMG	Leyland Tiger TRCTL11/3R	Plaxton Paramount 3200 III	C53F	1988	
d 109	E881YKY	Leyland Tiger TRCTL11/3RZ	Plaxton Paramount 3200 III	C53F	1988	
d 110	E882YKY	Leyland Tiger TRCTL11/3RZ	Plaxton Paramount 3200 III	C53F	1988	
b 786	F756OJH	Volvo B10M-60	Jonckheere Jubilee P50	C53F	1989	Ex Alder Valley, 1992
b 788	F758OJH	Volvo B10M-60	Jonckheere Jubilee P50	C53F	1989	Ex Alder Valley, 1992
b 789	F759OJH	Volvo B10M-60	Jonckheere Jubilee P50	C53F	1989	Ex Alder Valley, 1992
b 782	F772OJH	Volvo B10M-60	Jonckheere Jubilee P50	C53F	1989	Ex Alder Valley, 1992
b 783	F773OJH	Volvo B10M-60	Jonckheere Jubilee P50	C53F	1989	Ex Alder Valley, 1992
a 327	H327UWR	Volvo B10M-60	Plaxton Paramount 3500 III	C50F	1991	Ex Wallace Arnold, Leeds, 1994
a 328	H328UWR	Volvo B10M-60	Plaxton Paramount 3500 III	C50F	1991	Ex Wallace Arnold, Leeds, 1994

Previous Registrations
GIL6253 D209LWX   HIL7595 E663UNE   OIB3510 EWW544Y
GIL6949 D210LWX   HIL7596 E31SBO   OIB3520 B270KPF
GIL8487 E32SBO   HIL7597 E660UNE   OIB3521 B271KPF
GIL8488 E38SBO   IIL4579 E33SBO   OIB3522 B272KPF
HIL7594 E662UNE   IIL4580 E37SBO   OIB3523 B275KPF

Liveries
Many are expected to have gained the new revised Green Line livery by early 1995.
However, at the time of going to press, these were the liveries carried.
Bee Line (Yellow): 719, 727, 752.
New Green Line Livery: 116, 117, 129, 132, 133, 191, 724, 726, 728, 761, 762, 765-9, TDL53, TDL54, TDL55, ≤TDL60, TDL63, TDL65, TP1, TP13, TP61, TP70, TP71, TP72, TP75, TPL50-2, TPL55, TPL57, TPL84, TPL92, ≤TPL93, TPL510.
New Green Line Livery with London Link logos: 782, 786, 788.
New Green Line Livery with route 415 branding: 373 - 377.
Jetlink: 327, 328, 359, BTL47-9.
London Link: 754, 783, 789.
Old Green Line: 115, NTL5, TP15, TP36, TPL53, TPL98.
Luton & District (Red): 109-113, 118, 120, 122.

Most of the coaches operated by Bee Line on their Green Line routes now carry this attractive new livery in common with Countybus and Luton & District. Formerly TPL 95 in the L & D fleet, 767 is a daily visitor to the metropolis connecting London with Windsor on route 702. It is seen turning into Elizabeth Bridge, Victoria in August 1994. Colin Lloyd

Countybus route 711 has been running more or less unchanged for many years. One of the usual vehicles linking London with Harlow is TDL 55, a Duple 320 bodied Leyland Tiger acquired in 1993 from London & Country. It is wearing dedicated livery for route 724. Colin Lloyd

Representing the latest additions to the fleet of London & Country subsidiary Guildford & West Surrey is this dual purpose Greenway National. Marketed under the Green Line banner, they carry route branding for route 415 and link London with Guildford. November 1994 sees No.374 in Kingston. Geoff Rixon

The London Link motorway express service is operated by Bee Line with coaches painted in an adaption of the new Green Line livery. Nearing the end of its journey in Buckingham Palace Road is No.724, a Plaxton Supreme bodied Leyland Tiger formerly NTL 3 with Luton & District. *Colin Lloyd*

Sovereign have a part share with Speedlink Airport Services on route 747 linking Heathrow with the other London Airports at Luton and Gatwick. Looking resplendent in full Jetlink livery at Heathrow in August 1994 is No.327, a 1991 example of a Plaxton Paramount 3500 bodied Leyland Tiger acquired from Wallace Arnold of Leeds. *Colin Lloyd*

GREY-GREEN

T.Cowie plc, 53-55 Stamford Hill, London, N16 5TD

Coach Fleet

101	B101XYH	Auwaerter Neoplan N722	Plaxton Paramount 4000	CH55/20DT	1984
102	B102XYH	Auwaerter Neoplan N722	Plaxton Paramount 4000	CH55/20DT	1985
103	C103CYE	Scania K112TR	Plaxton Paramount 4000 II	CH57/18DT	1985
874	C874CYX	Volvo B10M-61	Plaxton Paramount 3200 II	C53F	1986
875	C875CYX	Volvo B10M-61	Plaxton Paramount 3200 II	C53F	1986
876	C876CYX	Volvo B10M-61	Plaxton Paramount 3200 II	C53F	1986
877	C877CYX	Volvo B10M-61	Plaxton Paramount 3200 II	C53F	1986
879	D879FYL	Volvo B10M-61	Plaxton Paramount 3200 III	C53F	1987
880	D880FYL	Volvo B10M-61	Plaxton Paramount 3200 III	C53F	1987
881	D881FYL	Volvo B10M-61	Plaxton Paramount 3200 III	C53F	1987
882	D882FYL	Volvo B10M-61	Plaxton Paramount 3500 III	C49FT	1987
883	D883FYL	Volvo B10M-61	Plaxton Paramount 3500 III	C49FT	1987
884	D884FYL	Volvo B10M-61	Plaxton Paramount 3500 III	C53F	1987
891	E891KYW	Volvo B10M-61	Duple 320	C53F	1988
892	E892KYW	Volvo B10M-61	Duple 320	C53F	1988
893	E893KYW	Volvo B10M-61	Duple 320	C53F	1988
895	E895KYW	Scania K92CRB	Van Hool Alizee H	C53F	1988
896	E896KYW	Scania K92CRB	Van Hool Alizee H	C53F	1988
897	E897KYW	Scania K92CRB	Van Hool Alizee H	C53F	1988
898	E898KYW	Scania K92CRB	Van Hool Alizee H	C53F	1988
899	E899KYW	Volvo B10M-61	Van Hool Alizee H	C53F	1988
900	E900KYW	Volvo B10M-61	Van Hool Alizee H	C53F	1988
901	E901MUC	Volvo B10M-61	Van Hool Alizee H	C49FT	1988
902	E902MUC	Volvo B10M-61	Van Hool Alizee H	C49FT	1988
903	E903MUC	Volvo B10M-61	Van Hool Alizee H	C49FT	1988
904	E904MUC	Volvo B10M-61	Van Hool Alizee H	C49FT	1988
905	G905TYR	DAF MB230LB615	Van Hool Alizee H	C49FT	1990
906	G906TYR	DAF MB230LB615	Van Hool Alizee H	C49FT	1990
907	G907TYR	DAF MB230LB615	Van Hool Alizee H	C49FT	1990
908	G908TYR	DAF MB230LB615	Van Hool Alizee H	C49FT	1990
909	G909TYR	DAF MB230LB615	Van Hool Alizee H	C49FT	1990
910	G910TYR	DAF MB230LB615	Van Hool Alizee H	C49FT	1990
932	K932VCP	DAF MB230LTF615	Van Hool Alizee HE	C49FT	1993
933	K933VCP	DAF MB230LTF615	Van Hool Alizee HE	C49FT	1993
942	M942LYR	DAF SB3000WS601	Van Hool Alizee HE	C49FT	1994
943	M943LYR	DAF SB3000WS601	Van Hool Alizee HE	C49FT	1994

Livery
White with green and orange relief.

Special Liveries
Eurolines (White): 905-908, 932, 933, 942, 943.

Opposite **As well as being a major bus operator in London, the Cowie Group own Grey-Green coaches. Representing the oldest batch of single deck coaches is 874, one of the 1986 intake and still giving good service. Many of these vehicles are used on commuter services as depicted here in Whitehall in July 1994.** Geoff Rixon

Above **The newest vehicles to be purchased by Grey-Green arrived in 1994 bedecked in Eurolines livery, the network of Trans-European express routes. En route to Amsterdam is 943, one of many coaches now employed by various companies providing vehicles and staff on contract to the Euroline concern. Drummond Gate in London's fashionable Pimlico provides the setting in September 1994.** Colin Lloyd

GUIDELINE

Guideline Coaches Ltd, 63, North Road, South Wimbledon, London, SW19 1AQ

✗ 929ECH	Mercedes-Benz 0303/15R	Mercedes-Benz	C49FT	1985		
DBZ945	Mercedes-Benz 0303/15R	Mercedes-Benz	C49FT	1986	Ex Yeates, Loughborough (Demonstrator), 1987	

Previous Registration
929ECH	From New	DBZ945	D757XBC

Livery
Two tone blue and white.

HAMILTON

D.L. Bennett, 589-591 Uxbridge Road, Hayes End, Middx, UB4 8HP

HOI5709	Auwaerter Neoplan N216H	Auwaerter Jetliner		C49FT	1984	Ex Smith, Ford, 1984
✗ B940MKP	DAF MB200DKFL600	Van Hool Alizee H		C50FT	1984	Ex Knight, Sidcup, 1994
✗ A4HOU	Kassbohrer Setra S215HD	Kassbohrer Tornado		C49FT	1986	Ex Cavalier, West Molesey, 1993
E251PEL	Bedford Venturer YNV	Duple 320		C52FT	1988	Ex County of Avon, 1994
✗ E254PEL	Bedford Venturer YNV	Duple 320		C52FT	1988	Ex County of Avon, 1994
F69FMC	Mercedes-Benz 811D	Reeve Burgess Beaver		C25F	1988	Ex London Borough of Harrow, 1993
J412LLK	Sanos S315.21	FAP Charisma		C47FT	1992	
J413LLK	Sanos S315.21	FAP Charisma		C47FT	1992	
J602LLK	Sanos S315.21	FAP Charisma		C53F	1992	
K35PLO	Sanos S315.21	FAP Charisma		C47FT	1992	

Previous Registrations
HOI5709	B667DVL	A4HOU	D840XPJ	B940MKP	B360DWF, WOI504, WSV488

Liveries
Various different schemes.

Guideline operate a smart pair of integral Mercedes-Benz 0303s from their base in South Wimbledon. This one is 929ECH, purchased new in 1985 and cruising through Parliament Square in July 1994. Note the differences in trim between this and the David Corbel Sanos Charisma shown earlier. *Colin Lloyd*

With the railway signalmen on strike during August 1994, many extra vehicles were drafted onto the London-Gatwick 777 route to cover the lack of trains. One such coach was Hamilton of Uxbridge's E254PEL, a Bedford Venturer with Duple 320 body. It shows one of the many liveries used by Hamilton as it departs from Victoria Coach Station. *Colin Lloyd*

Hamilton operate a variety of coaches, but only one Kassbohrer Setra Tornado. On layover after working National Express route 201 from London is A4HOU in Cardiff Bus Station. A different livery is carried by each individual vehicle in this fleet. Richard Eversden

About to turn into Buckingham Palace Road from Eccleston Bridge on route 777, this DAF/Van Hool combination remains unique in Hamilton's operation. Colin Lloyd

HAMPTONS OF LONDON

Hampton Coaches (Westminster) Ltd, 54b Trundleys Road, London, SE8 5JG

WMA112M	Leyland Leopard PSU3B/4R	Plaxton Panorama Elite III Exp	C53F	1974	Ex Cocklin, London SE7, 1994
XEX160S	Bedford VAS5	Plaxton Supreme III	C29F	1978	Ex Norfolk, Great Yarmouth, 1980
ARF823T	Volvo B58-61	Duple Dominant II	C53F	1979	Ex Ashall, Levenshulme, 1992
EWW221T	Leyland Leopard PSU3E/4R	Duple Dominant II	C53F	1979	Ex Cocklin, London SE8, 1994
GGD672T	Volvo B58-61	Duple Dominant II	C57F	1979	Ex Cocklin, London SE8, 1994
YPL81T	AEC Reliance 6U2R	Duple Dominant II Express	C49F	1979	Ex Poulton, London SE16, 1994
XJG813V	Leyland Leopard PSU5C/4R	Duple Dominant I	C53F	1980	Ex Sykes, Appleton Roebuck, 1993
FHS769X	Volvo B10M-61	Duple Goldliner III	C53F	1982	Ex McColl, Balloch, 1992
MYX32X	Bedford YNT	Duple Dominant	C53F	1982	Ex Golden Travel, London W10, 1988
UYA699	Volvo B10M-61	Duple Goldliner IV	C51FT	1982	Ex Tentrek, Sidcup, 1987
WSV504	Bedford YMP	Plaxton Paramount 3200	C31F	1984	Ex Plumpton, Plumpton Green, 1990
YMA696	Volvo B10M-61	Plaxton Paramount 3500	C51FT	1984	Ex Transcity, Sidcup, 1989
A77JWD	Ford R1115	Duple Dominant IV	C53F	1984	Ex Bennett, Gloucester, 1988
955HUS	Scania K112CRS	Jonckheere Jubilee P599	C51FT	1984	Ex Golden, London W10, 1988
119UYA	Bedford YNT	Plaxton Paramount 3200 II	C53F	1985	Ex Willetts, Yorkley, 1991

Previous Registrations

119UYA	B105PJF	WSV504	A954FNJ		ARF823T	EWW224T, PNH182
955HUS	B70MLT, B398PLU	YMA696	A764HGX		MYX32X	248D240
UYA699	VGU907X					

Livery
Two tone blue with grey relief.

Very often, a coach as manoeuvrable as this small Bedford YMP can be very handy in London's congested streets. As clearly shown in this view of Hampton's WSV504, the tiny feature window was omitted from the short wheelbase Plaxton Paramount. Colin Lloyd

HARDINGS

D.J. & J.S. Harding, Wellwood, Wellhouse Lane, Betchworth, Surrey, RH3 7HH

TPJ270S	Bedford YMT	Plaxton Supreme III	C53F	1977	
A399NNK	Mercedes-Benz L309D	Reeve Burgess	M12	1983	
HCT554	Kassbohrer Setra S215HR	Kassbohrer Rational	C53F	1984	Ex Premier-Albanian, Watford, 1985
NSU496	Volvo B10M-61	Van Hool Alizee	C53F	1985	Ex Shearings, Wigan, 1990
NSU137	Volvo B10M-61	Van Hool Alizee	C53F	1986	Ex Shearings, Wigan, 1991
D338DPL	Kassbohrer Setra S215HD	Kassbohrer Tornado	C49FT	1987	Ex Loveridge, Marks Tey, 1989
E989NMK	Mercedes-Benz 609D	Reeve Burgess Beaver	C25F	1988	
E589VTH	Volvo B10M-61	Plaxton Paramount 3500 III	C53F	1988	Ex Shearings, Wigan, 1990
F468SPH	Mercedes-Benz 811D	Reeve Burgess Beaver	C25F	1989	
L2HCT	Mercedes-Benz 711D	Plaxton Beaver	C25F	1994	
L690RNW	Mercedes-Benz 410D	Autobus Classique	C16F	1994	

Previous Registrations
HCT554	A246GPL	NSU496	B479UNB		E589VTH	E589VTH, NSU137
NSU137	C527DND	D338DPL	D735BPC, NSU137			

Livery
White with red and orange relief.

HAROLD WOOD COACHES

F.W. Leach, 12 Woodlands Road, Harold Wood, Essex, RM3 0RA

HIL7197	Bedford YLQ	Plaxton Supreme IV	C45F	1979	
HIL7196	Bedford YLQ	Plaxton Supreme IV	C45F	1980	
HIL7195	Bedford YLQ	Plaxton Supreme IV	C45F	1981	
B291AMG	Leyland Tiger TRCTL11/3RZ	Plaxton Paramount 3500 II	C57F	1985	Named Euro IV
C391DML	Leyland Tiger TRCTL11/3RZ	Plaxton Paramount 3500 II	C53F	1985	Named Euro V
D123HMH	Volvo B10M-61	Plaxton Paramount 3500 II	C53F	1986	Named Euro I
D124HMH	Volvo B10M-61	Plaxton Paramount 3500 II	C53F	1986	Named Euro II
G915WAY	Volvo B10M-60	Caetano Algarve	C57F	1990	Named Euro VII
L59YJF	Volvo B10M-62	Caetano Algarve II	C49FT	1994	

Previous Registrations
HIL7195	HMU425W	HIL7196	CMT919V	HIL7197	CMJ460T

Livery
Cream with orange and two tone blue relief.

HARRIS COACHES

Frank Harris (Coaches) Ltd, Manor Road, West Thurrock, Essex, RM16 1EH

Coach Fleet

6306FH	DAF SB2300DKSB585	Van Hool Alizee H	C48FT	1985
9242FH	Scania K112TRS	Plaxton Paramount 4000 II	CH54/18CT	1985
2942FH	Bova FHD12.280	Bova Futura	C53F	1986
7968FH	DAF SB3000DKV601	Van Hool Alizee H	C49FT	1988
5970FH	DAF SB3000DKV601	Van Hool Alizee H	C49FT	1988
8947FH	DAF SB3000DKV601	Van Hool Alizee H	C49FT	1988
1245FH	DAF SB3000DKV601	Van Hool Alizee H	C49FT	1989
FHV504	DAF SB3000DKV601	Van Hool Alizee H	C49FT	1989
J91WWC	Kassboher Setra S215HD	Kassbohrer Tornado	C49FT	1991
J92YAR	Kassboher Setra S215HD	Kassbohrer Tornado	C49FT	1991
K95GEV	DAF SB3000DKVF601	Van Hool Alizee HE	C48FT	1993
K96GEV	DAF SB3000DKVF601	Van Hool Alizee HE	C48FT	1993
K97GEV	DAF SB3000DKVF601	Van Hool Alizee HE	C48FT	1993
K122OCT	Kassboher Setra S215HD	Kassbohrer Tornado	C49FT	1993
K123OCT	Kassboher Setra S215HD	Kassbohrer Tornado	C49FT	1993
L93OAR	Auwaerter Neoplan N112/3	Auwaerter Skyliner	CH54/16CT	1994
L97PTW	Toyota HZB50R	Caetano Optimo III	C21F	1994
L98PTW	Toyota HZB50R	Caetano Optimo III	C21F	1994

Previous Registrations
1245FH	F98RAR	6306FH	B89CNO	9242FH	C400JOO
2942FH	C90LVX	7968FH	E95EVW	FHV504	F99RAR
5970FH	E96EVW	8947FH	F97MHJ		

The Kassbohrer Setra features twice in the Hardings of Betchworth operation; the older of the two is this French built Rational model. Passing the public entrance to the Houses of Parliament in St Margaret Street is HCT554. Note the large number of constituents in the background queuing up to lobby their respective MPs in June 1994. *Colin Lloyd*

The Beaver body has obviously found favour with Hardings of Betchworth with three in the fleet; two are of Reeve Burgess parentage and the third a Plaxton. Representing one of the former is F468SPH mounted on the Mercedes-Benz 811 chassis. *Colin Lloyd*

All vehicles in the fleet of Harold Wood Coaches were purchased new. D123HMH is a Volvo B10M with Plaxton Paramount 3500 II body of 1986 vintage, seen in far-away Southwold, Suffolk in September 1994. *Geoff Mills*

Sunny June 1994 and Harris of Grays 7968FH is turning into Elizabeth Bridge, Victoria. Half of the coach fleet is made up of the DAF SB/Van Hool Alizee as depicted here. *Colin Lloyd*

HEARN'S / VENTURE

R. Hearn, 801 Kenton Lane, Harrow, Middx, HA3 6AH

Venture Transport (Hendon) (1965) Ltd, 331 Pinner Road, Harrow, Middx, HA1 4HF

Hearn's fleet

HIL5875	Leyland Leopard PSU3C/4R	Plaxton Panorama Elite III	C53F	1975	Ex Horlock, Northfleet, 1978
HIL8573	Leyland Leopard PSU3C/4R	Duple Dominant	C51F	1976	Ex Cavalier, Hounslow, 1978
HIL5876	Leyland Leopard PSU3C/4R	Plaxton Supreme III	C51F	1978	
HIL2153	Leyland Leopard PSU5C/4R	Plaxton Supreme IV	C57F	1979	
HIL2154	Leyland Leopard PSU5C/4R	Plaxton Supreme IV	C57F	1979	
HIL2156	Leyland Leopard PSU3E/4R	Plaxton Supreme IV	C53F	1980	
HIL2155	Leyland Leopard PSU3E/4R	Plaxton Supreme IV	C53F	1982	
968KUR	Leyland Tiger TRCTL11/2R	Plaxton Supreme V	C53F	1982	Ex Rover, Chesham, 1992
LVG878	Leyland Tiger TRCTL11/3R	Plaxton Paramount 3500	C50F	1983	
HIL2157	Leyland Tiger TRCTL11/3R	Plaxton Paramount 3200	C57F	1984	Ex Ebdon, Sidcup, 1986
HIL2158	Leyland Tiger TRCTL11/3R	Plaxton Paramount 3200	C57F	1984	Ex The Londoners, London SE15, 1986
HIL2159	Leyland Tiger TRCTL11/3R	Plaxton Paramount 3200 II	C55F	1985	Ex Armchair, Brentford, 1986
X HIL2160	Leyland Tiger TRCTL11/3R	Plaxton Paramount 3200 II	C57F	1985	Ex Armchair, Brentford, 1986
HIL2385	Bedford YNT	Plaxton Paramount 3200 III	C53F	1987	Ex Owen, Yateley, 1993
SJI7046	Bedford YNT	Plaxton Paramount 3200 III	C53F	1987	Ex Owen, Yateley, 1993
SJI7418	Mercedes-Benz 307D	Reeve Burgess	M12	1987	
SJI7415	Leyland Tiger TRCTL11/3ARZ	Plaxton Paramount 3200 III	C55F	1988	Ex Armchair, Brentford, 1993
SJI7416	Leyland Tiger TRCTL11/3ARZ	Plaxton Paramount 3200 III	C55F	1988	Ex Armchair, Brentford, 1993
HIL8518	Leyland Tiger TRCTL11/3ARZ	Plaxton Paramount 3200 III	C57F	1988	
HIL8519	Leyland Tiger TRCTL11/3ARZ	Plaxton Paramount 3200 III	C57F	1988	
SJI7049	Volvo B10M-60	Plaxton Paramount 3200 III	C53F	1989	Ex Frames Rickards, London WC1, 1994
SJI7054	Volvo B10M-60	Plaxton Paramount 3200 III	C53F	1989	Ex Frames Rickards, London WC1, 1994

Venture Travel fleet

HIL6143	Leyland Leopard PSU3C/4R	Plaxton Supreme III	C44F	1976	
HIL8251	Leyland Leopard PSU3C/4R	Plaxton Supreme III	C53F	1976	
HIL8309	Leyland Leopard PSU5A/4R	Plaxton Supreme III	C57F	1976	
HIL8548	Leyland Leopard PSU5A/4R	Plaxton Supreme III	C57F	1976	
HIL4415	Leyland Leopard PSU3E/4R	Plaxton Supreme IV	C44F	1979	Ex Hearn, Harrow Weald, 1990
HIL4436	Leyland Leopard PSU5C/4R	Plaxton Supreme IV	C57F	1979	
HIL5952	Leyland Leopard PSU3E/4R	Plaxton Supreme IV	C44F	1979	
X HIL5953	Leyland Leopard PSU5C/4R	Plaxton Supreme IV	C57F	1979	
HIL3807	Leyland Tiger TRCTL11/3R	Plaxton Paramount 3200	C55F	1983	Ex Premier-Albanian, Watford, 1987
HIL8907	Volvo B10M-61	Plaxton Paramount 3500	C50F	1983	Ex Epsom Coaches, 1992
HIL8984	Volvo B10M-61	Plaxton Paramount 3500	C50F	1983	Ex Epsom Coaches, 1992
HIL2173	Leyland Tiger TRCTL11/3R	Plaxton Paramount 3200 II	C55F	1985	Ex Armchair, Brentford, 1986
D546KMG	Volvo B10M-61	Plaxton Paramount 3200 III	C53F	1987	Ex Frames Rickards, London WC1, 1994
D547KMG	Volvo B10M-61	Plaxton Paramount 3200 III	C53F	1987	Ex Frames Rickards, London WC1, 1994
M590GRY	Toyota Coaster HZB50R	Caetano Optimo III	C21F	1994	

Previous Registrations

968KUR	DNK590Y	HIL4415	GBM124T	HIL8548	NNK813P
HIL2153	GBM122T	HIL4436	GBM127T	HIL8573	SUR292R
HIL2154	GBM123T	HIL5875	MKJ252P	HIL8907	NGT303Y
HIL2155	ANK315X	HIL5876	VMJ964S	HIL8984	NGT304Y
HIL2156	PRO441W	HIL5952	GBM125T	LVG878	A387NNK
HIL2157	A193RUR	HIL5953	GBM126T	SJI7046	E829EUT, OVK902, E848KCF
HIL2158	A194RUR	HIL6143	NNK810P	SJI7049	F891SMU
HIL2159	B401CMC	HIL8251	NNK811P	SJI7054	F889SMU
HIL2160	B402CMC	HIL8309	NNK812P	SJI7415	E994NMK
HIL2173	B403CMC	HIL8518	E318OMG	SJI7416	E995NMK
HIL2385	D390BNR	HIL8519	E319OMG	SJI7418	E42MMT
HIL3807	KBM103Y				

Liveries

Hearn's: Grey, light blue and white.
Venture: Yellow and black.

HILLS OF HERSHAM

D. Hill, 129 Burwood Road, Hersham, Surrey, KT12 4QN

GHM882N	Daimler Fleetline CRL6	MCW	H44/24D	1975	Ex Horsham Coaches, Warnham, 1994
JTN653P	Bedford VAS5	Plaxton Supreme III	C29F	1976	Ex Gateway, Chertsey, 1992
CSR516V	Ford R1114	Plaxton Supreme IV	C53F	1980	Ex Coston, Gatwick, 1994
PRO437W	Bedford YMT	Plaxton Supreme IV	C53F	1980	Ex Wentworth Coaches, Virginia Water, 1994
OWV819	Bedford YMQ	Plaxton Supreme IV	C26F	1981	Ex Spirit of London, Hounslow, 1990
✗ TSV806	Volvo B10M-61	Jonckheere Bermuda	C49FT	1982	Ex Williamson, Christchurch, 1991
KNP1X	Volvo B10M-56	Plaxton Viewmaster IV Express	C45FT	1982	Ex Bailey, Sutton-in-Ashfield, 1992
CBA215Y	Ford Transit	Mellor	C16F	1983	Ex M & E Coaches, Hersham, 1991
DFP532Y	DAF MB200DKTL600	Jonckheere Jubilee P50	C51FT	1983	Ex Stirk, Torquay, 1993
✗ 790LKR	Volvo B10M-61	Jonckheere Jubilee P90	CH49/9FT	1983	Ex North Mymms, Potters Bar, 1993
KIW3080	Leyland TigerTRCTL11/3R	Plaxton Paramount 3500	C51FT	1984	Ex Wessex, Bristol, 1992
823NMC	Volvo B10M-61	Van Hool Alizee H	C49FT	1984	Ex Admiral, Welwyn Garden City, 1993
B624HFW	ACE Puma	Van Hool Alizee	C30F	1985	Ex LW Tours, London N2, 1994
C539GPP	Ford Transit	Chassis Developments	C16F	1986	Ex Gateway, Chertsey, 1992
C806TLF	Bedford YMP	Plaxton Paramount 3200 II	C35F	1986	Ex Marton, West Drayton, 1991
D324WPE	Ford Transit 190D	Carlyle	B16F	1986	Ex Alder Valley, 1991
D330WPE	Ford Transit 190D	Carlyle	B16F	1986	Ex BTB, Hersham, 1992
D334WPE	Ford Transit 190D	Carlyle	B16F	1986	Ex Alder Valley, 1991
D344WPE	Ford Transit 190D	Carlyle	B16F	1986	Ex Alder Valley, 1991
E844JLT	Ford Transit	Ford	M12	1988	Ex private owner, 1993
G280BEL	Dennis Javelin 12SDA1907	Caetano Algarve	C51FT	1989	Ex Manning, Challow, 1994
G281BEL	Dennis Javelin 12SDA1907	Caetano Algarve	C53F	1989	Ex Manning, Challow, 1994
G590PKK	Renault Master T35D	Crystals	M15	1989	
G947VBC	Toyota Coaster HB31R	Caetano Optimo	C21F	1989	Ex Connoisseur, London NW10, 1993
G498GJC	Leyland DAF 400	Leyland DAF	C16F	1990	Ex Wardell, Prestatyn, 1992
✗ J541AWW	Renault Master B110	Central Coachcraft	C16F	1991	
L665CNA	Ford Transit	Deansgate	C16F	1993	

Previous Registrations						
790LKR	MRP839Y	OWV819	UUR843W, XWO895, AGP527W		DFP532Y	5551PP, 1379PP
823NMC	A601UGD	TSV806	ENV826X		B624HFW	B638MSF, GSU379
KIW3080	A381AKW					

Livery
White and red.

HOUSTON & BRYANT

J.R. Houston & L.R. Bryant, Boundary Garage, 38 Crawley Road, Wood Green, London, N22 6AN

BBM77A	Volvo B10M-61	Jonckheere Bermuda	C49FT	1980	Ex Renyard, Totton, 1987
YSV738	Leyland Leopard PSU5D/4R	Plaxton Supreme V	C53F	1981	Ex Wessex, Bristol, 1990
LUA272V	Leyland Leopard PSU3F/4R	Plaxton Supreme IV	C53F	1981	Ex Cottrell, Mitcheldean, 1989
TND414X	DAF MB200DKTL600	Plaxton Supreme V	C51F	1982	Ex Buzz, Harlow, 1993
DNK583Y	Bristol LHS6L	Plaxton Supreme V	C35F	1983	Ex Heaney, Enfield, 1993
B251AMG	Bedford YNT	Plaxton Paramount 3200	C53F	1984	Ex Angel Motors, London N15, 1989
C980NFW	Mercedes-Benz L608D	Coachcraft	C21F	1986	
✗ C593VUT	DAF SB2300DHS585	Smit Orion	C53FT	1986	Ex Daniels, Abridge, 1992
D881ALN	Mercedes-Benz 609D	Coachcraft	C21FL	1986	
E478GBV	Mercedes-Benz 609D	Reeve Burgess	C19F	1987	Ex East Pennine, Halifax, 1990
E795KCR	Talbot Freeway	Talbot	B16F	1987	Ex Sochulbus, Ashford, 1993
E321KKV	Talbot Freeway	Talbot	B16FL	1988	Ex Coventry City Council, 1994
E364KKV	Talbot Freeway	Talbot	B16FL	1988	Ex Sochulbus, Ashford, 1993
E38YDO	Mercedes-Benz 609D	Advanced Vehicle Builders	C21F	1988	
F679FFJ	Talbot Freeway	Talbot	B16FL	1988	Ex Clintona, Long Melford, 1993
F590HUS	Talbot Freeway	Talbot	B12FL	1989	Ex McDade, Uddingston, 1994
F591HUS	Talbot Freeway	Talbot	B12FL	1989	Ex McDade, Uddingston, 1994
F488VRP	Iveco 49.10	Leicester Carriage Builders	B13FL	1989	Ex Northampton County Council, 1993
G346EOK	Leyland-DAF 400	Jubilee	B14FL	1990	Ex private owner, 1994
G54GBD	Leyland-DAF 400	Crystals	B12FL	1990	Ex private owner, 1993
G939AAY	Leyland-DAF 400	Walsall Conversions (1994)	B16FL	1990	Ex private owner, 1993
H649COD	Leyland-DAF 400	Zodiac (1993)	B12FL	1991	Ex private owner, 1993
J906BUA	Leyland-DAF 400	Crystals	M16	19..	Ex Cropper, Leeds, 1994
J769NHA	Leyland-DAF 400	Jubilee	M16	19..	Ex Fairway, Hull, 1994
L764KWL	Leyland-DAF 400	Walsall Conversions	M16L	1994	

Livery	Previous Registrations			
White with yellow and green relief.	BBM77A	WNH823W	YSV738	SND292X

"The falling leaves.." and Hearn's Leyland Tiger rests sedately in the autumn sunshine at Hampton Court Green in November 1994. New in 1985 to Armchair, this vehicle was acquired in 1986 by the present owner.
Geoff Rixon

Venture currently have eight Leyland Leopards on their books, all with Plaxton Supreme bodies. Shown here is a 12-metre PSU5 type which has the IV variant of the Supreme design. HIL5953 arrives at the Epsom Derby fully laden with passengers looking forward to a good day at the races.
Keith Grimes

Scarce within the London operating area is this deck-and-a-half bodied Jonckheere Jubilee P90 owned by Hills of Hersham. November 1994 sees this superbly kept example about to depart its Byfleet home on another private hire.
Geoff Rixon

Of the imported stock owned by Hills of Hersham, this Jonckheere Bermuda bodied Volvo B10M is the oldest. Still in fine condition for a 1982 coach, albeit freshly repainted, it is pictured in Byfleet glistening in the November sunshine.
Geoff Rixon

Not a common sight in the Metropolis are Renault minicoaches. With bodywork supplied by Central Coachcraft, Hills of Hersham own two examples, the newer one being J541AWW seen here negotiating Parliament Square in November 1994.
Colin Lloyd

Without doubt, one of the rarest types of bodywork to be seen in Britain is the Smit. One of only ten Smit bodied vehicles sold to British operators, C593VUT is still in daily service with Houston & Bryant of Wood Green. This is the Orion design, one of the three types sold in the UK.
Colin Lloyd

A former Park's of Hamilton coach, G66 RGG is now with Ideal Services of Watford. As is the norm in this fleet, it has a Plaxton Paramount 3500 III body. As with most of the fleet, no fleetnames are carried as in this view taken in Oxford Street in July 1994. Colin Lloyd

IDEAL SERVICES

Ideal Services Ltd, 34 Marythorne Close, Watford, Herts, WD1 7JU

F416DUG	Volvo B10M-60	Plaxton Paramount 3500 III	C50F	1989	Ex Trueman, Camberley, 1994
F975HGE	Volvo B10M-60	Plaxton Paramount 3500 III	C49FT	1989	Ex R & I, London NW10, 1994
✗ G66RGG	Volvo B10M-60	Plaxton Paramount 3500 III	C53F	1990	Ex Redwing, London SE5, 1994
H787RWJ	Scania K113CRB	Plaxton Paramount 3500 III	C53F	1991	Ex Redwing, London SE5, 1994

Livery
White.
H787RWJ carries Redwing fleetnames.

IMPACT

A.Hill, 46 Drayton Park Road, London, W13 8RY

DNC990Y	Volkswagen LT28	Cheshire Continental	M12	1981	Ex Ashall, Fallowfield, 1986
GSU382	Volvo B10M-61	Jonkheere Bermuda	C51FT	1982	Ex Scancoaches, London NW10, 1990
C567XLK	Ford Transit	Deansgate	M12	1986	Ex Wings, Hayes, 1989
D219NUR	Ford Transit	Chassis Developments	C16F	1986	
ONT46	Volvo B10M-61	Jonkheere Jubilee P599	C51FT	1988	Ex Globeheath, Cardiff, 1991
F113SFB	Mercedes-Benz 609D	Made-To-Measure	C26F	1989	
F135UMD	Leyland Swift LBM6T/2RSO	Reeve Burgess Harrier	C37F	1989	
✗ G652UHU	Mercedes-Benz 609D	Made-To-Measure	C26F	1989	
G171XHU	Mercedes-Benz 609D	Made-To-Measure	C26F	1990	
H187CVU	Mercedes-Benz 609D	Made-To-Measure	C24F	1990	
H207CVU	Talbot Express	Made-To-Measure	M12	1990	
H208CVU	Talbot Express	Made-To-Measure	M12	1990	
H413DVM	DAF 400	Made-To-Measure	C16F	1991	
H415DVM	Mercedes-Benz 609D	Made-To-Measure	C24F	1991	
L402CND	DAF 400	Concept	C16FL	1993	
L551CND	DAF 400	Concept	C16F	1993	
L552CND	DAF 400	Concept	C16F	1993	
L553CND	DAF 400	Concept	C16F	1993	
L554CND	DAF 400	Concept	C16F	1993	
L232DNC	Talbot Express	Concept	M12	1993	
L233DNC	Talbot Express	Concept	M12	1993	
L234DNC	Talbot Express	Concept	M12	1993	
L436CND	DAF 400	Concept	C16F	1994	
L195SCM	Mercedes-Benz 609D	Concept	C24F	1994	
L402CND	DAF 400	Concept	C16FL	1994	
M461NDB	LDV 400	LDV	C16F	1994	
M652NDB	LDV 400	LDV	C16F	1994	
M749WCM	Mercedes-Benz 609D	North West Coach Sales	C24F	1994	

Previous Registrations

GSU382	JNV629Y	C567XLK	C334DVU, WET342	ONT46	E208GNV

Livery
White with magenta signwriting.

Impact operate a considerable fleet with minicoaches being in the majority. A typical example is this Mercedes-Benz 609D with Made-To-Measure 26-seat bodywork. A sunny Hampton Court Road in June 1994 finds **G652UHU.** Geoff Rixon

THE ISLEWORTH

A.C. & D.F. Blackford, 45 Hall Road, Isleworth, TW7 7PA

✗ 4426BY	Volvo B58-61		Plaxton Viewmaster IV	C40FT	1981	Ex Len Wright, Isleworth, 1986
1957BY	Volvo B58-61		Plaxton Viewmaster IV	C53F	1981	Ex Fountain, Twickenham, 1990
LJI8027	Volvo B10M-61		Duple Dominant III	C49FT	1981	Ex Hurst & Leeke, Goose Green, 1993
UPG498	Volvo B10M-61		Plaxton Paramount 3500	C53F	1984	Ex Price Global, Hounslow, 1994

Previous Registrations

1957BY	SLH4W	LJI8027	BKF348X
4426BY	SLH1W	UPG498	A702XMH

Livery
Blue, red and grey with white relief.

A distinctive vehicle in The Isleworth operation is 4426BY. Mounted on a Volvo B58, it has the uncommon Plaxton Viewmaster coachwork plus tables and lamps fitted to the third and fourth bays. Colin Lloyd

67

KENTISH BUS & COACH

Kentish Bus & Coach Company Ltd, Apex House, London Road, Northfleet, Kent, DA11 9PD

Coach Fleet

9	TIB5905	Leyland Tiger TRCTL11/3R	Duple 320	C53F	1986	
10	TIB5906	Leyland Tiger TRCTL11/3R	Duple 320	C51F	1986	
11	C256SPC	Leyland Tiger TRCTL11/3RH	Duple 320	C53F	1986	Ex London & Country, 1994
17	XSV689	Leyland Tiger TRCTL11/3RH	Plaxton Paramount 3500 II	C49F	1985	
18	XSV691	Leyland Tiger TRCTL11/3RH	Plaxton Paramount 3500 II	C49F	1985	
19	XSV262	Leyland Tiger TRCTL11/3RH	Berkhof Everest 370	C49FT	1984	
21	KBC193	Leyland Tiger TRCTL11/3RH	Berkhof Everest 370	C49FT	1986	
27	OSK776	Leyland Tiger TRCTL11/3RH	Berkhof Everest 370	C49FT	1986	
28	YYB122	Leyland Tiger TRCTL11/3RH	Berkhof Everest 370	C49FT	1986	
29	JSK994	Leyland Tiger TRCTL11/3RH	Berkhof Everest 370	C49FT	1986	
30	TIB5903	Volvo B10M-61	Van Hool Alizee	C53F	1988	Ex Jasons, Orpington, 1993
31	TIB5904	Volvo B10M-61	Van Hool Alizee	C53F	1988	Ex Jasons, Orpington, 1993
32	HIL2279	Volvo B10M-61	Plaxton Paramount 3500 III	C50F	1987	Ex Wallace Arnold, Leeds, 1993
33	TIB5901	Volvo B10M-61	Plaxton Paramount 3500 III	C50F	1987	Ex Wallace Arnold, Leeds, 1993
34	A14GTA	Volvo B10M-60	Plaxton Paramount 3500 III	C53F	1990	Ex Park's, Hamilton, 1994
35	A11GTA	Volvo B10M-60	Plaxton Paramount 3500 III	C53F	1991	Ex Park's, Hamilton, 1994
36	E91OJT	Leyland Tiger TRCTL11/3ZR	Plaxton Paramount 3200 II	C53F	1988	Ex London & Country, 1994

Named Vehicles
9 Silver Lining 27 Silver Bullet 30 Silver Fox
19 Silver Jubilee 28 Silver Sprite 31 Silver Link
21 Silver Belle

Previous Registrations
HIL2279	E300UUB		TIB5903	E316OPR		XSV689	C202PPE
JSK994	C153SPB		TIB5904	E319OPR		XSV691	C204PPE
KBC193	B118KPF		TIB5905	C261SPC		YYB122	C152SPB
OSK776	C150SPB		TIB5906	C264SPC		A11GTA	H832AHS
TIB5901	E301UUB, HIL2280, E648WWU		XSV262	B114KPF		A14GTA	G89RGG

Liveries
White (GTA fleetnames);- 10, 32-5.
Kentish Express (Silver and maroon);- 9, 19, 21, 27-31.
White (Kentish Express logos);- 17, 18.

Kentish Bus & Coach no longer operate a Green Line route as such; route 720 between Victoria and Gravesend is now marketed as a Kentish Express route. Among the varied assortment of vehicles to be seen on this route is No.30, a Van Hool Alizee bodied Volvo B10M-61. July 1994 finds this former Jasons of Orpington coach leaving Buckingham Palace Road en route to Gravesend. Colin Lloyd

THE KINGS FERRY

P.S. O'Neill, The Coach Station, Pump Lane, Gillingham, Kent, ME8 7TJ

2.1	K13KFC	Toyota Coaster HDB30R	Caetano Optimo II	C21F	1992	Ex Allison's, Dunfermline, 1993
2.2	H10KFC	Toyota Coaster HDB30R	Caetano Optimo II	C21F	1991	
3.1	M3KFC	MAN 11.190HOCLR	Berkhof Excellence 1000	C33FT	1994	
3.2	H8KFC	MAN 11.180HOCL	Berkhof Excellence 1000	C33FT	1991	
3.3	L3KFC	MAN 11.190HOCLR	Berkhof Excellence 1000	C33FT	1993	
3.4	L4KFC	MAN 11.190HOCLR	Berkhof Excellence 1000	C33FT	1993	
4.1	GIL8490	Mercedes-Benz 0303/15	Mercedes-Benz	C49FT	1988	Ex Scarlet Band, West Cornforth, 1991
4.2	H2KFC	Mercedes-Benz 0303/2	Mercedes-Benz	C49FT	1991	
4.3	H3KFC	Mercedes-Benz 0303/2	Mercedes-Benz	C49FT	1991	
4.4	H4KFC	Mercedes-Benz 0303/2	Mercedes-Benz	C49FT	1991	
4.5	H5KFC	Mercedes-Benz 0303/2	Mercedes-Benz	C49FT	1991	
4.6	H6KFC	Mercedes-Benz 0303/2	Mercedes-Benz	C49FT	1991	
4.7	RJI2713	Kassbohrer S215HD	Kassbohrer Tornado	C49FT	1990	Ex Hallmark, Luton, 1994
4.8	RJI2714	Kassbohrer S215HD	Kassbohrer Tornado	C49FT	1990	Ex Hallmark, Luton, 1994
4.9	K5KFC	Scania K113CRB	Berkhof Excellence 2000HL	C49FT	1993	
4.10	H155RHE	Auwaerter Neoplan N116/3	Auwaerter Cityliner	C48FT	1990	Ex Parry, Cheslyn Hay, 1994
4.11	K6KFC	Scania K113CRB	Berkhof Excellence 2000	C49FT	1993	
4.12	J4KFC	Scania K113CRB	Berkhof Excellence 2000	C49FT	1992	
4.13	J5KFC	Scania K113CRB	Berkhof Excellence 2000	C49FT	1992	
4.14	J6KFC	Scania K113CRB	Berkhof Excellence 2000	C49FT	1992	
4.18	KIB545	Volvo B10M-60	Berkhof Excellence 2000	C49FT	1990	Ex Gale, Haslemere, 1992
4.19	K7KFC	Scania K113CRB	Berkhof Excellence 2000	C49FT	1993	
4.20	K8KFC	Scania K113CRB	Berkhof Excellence 2000	C49FT	1993	
4.21	H11KFC	Auwaerter Neoplan N116/3	Auwaerter Cityliner	C49FT	1990	Ex Happy Days, Woodseaves, 1993
4.22	L8KFC	Bova FHD12.340	Bova Futura	C51FT	1994	
4.23	M2KFC	Scania K113CRB	Irizar Century	C49FT	1994	
4.24	H17KFC	Mercedes-Benz 0303	Plaxton Paramount 3500 III	C49FT	1991	
4.25	H18KFC	Mercedes-Benz 0303	Plaxton Paramount 3500 III	C49FT	1991	
4.26	A14KFC	Auwaerter Neoplan N116/3	Auwaerter Cityliner	C48FT	1990	Ex Parry, Cheslyn Hay, 1993
5.1	A18KFC	Bova FHD12.290	Bova Futura	C55F	1990	
5.2	A19KFC	Bova FHD12.290	Bova Futura	C55F	1990	
5.3	GIL2784	Bova FHD12.290	Bova Futura	C55F	1990	
5.4	L6KFC	Bova FHD12.340	Bova Futura	C55F	1994	
5.5	GIL2786	Bova FHD12.290	Bova Futura	C55F	1990	
5.6	H14KFC	Mercedes-Benz 0303	Plaxton Paramount 3500 III	C53F	1991	
5.7	H16KFC	Mercedes-Benz 0303	Plaxton Paramount 3500 III	C53F	1991	
5.8	H19KFC	Mercedes-Benz 0303	Plaxton Paramount 3500 III	C53F	1991	
5.9	K12KFC	Dennis Javelin 12SDA2117	Berkhof Excellence 1000	C53F	1993	
5.11	H20KFC	Mercedes-Benz 0303	Plaxton Paramount 3500 III	C53F	1991	
5.12	L7KFC	Bova FHD12.340	Bova Futura	C55F	1994	
5.14	J7KFC	Mercedes-Benz 0303	Plaxton Paramount 3500 III	C53F	1992	
5.15	J8KFC	Mercedes-Benz 0303	Plaxton Paramount 3500 III	C53F	1992	
7.1	K14KFC	Scania K113TRB	Berkhof Excellence 2000HD	CH57/19CT	1993	
7.2	K15KFC	Scania K113TRB	Berkhof Excellence 2000HD	CH57/19CT	1993	
7.3	L5KFC	Scania K113TRA	Berkhof Excellence 2000HD	CH57/23CT	1994	
7.4	M4KFC	Scania K113TRA	Berkhof Excellence 2000HD	CH57/23CT	1994	
	H20VCC	Ford Transit	Asquith	C11F	1991	Ex Vintage Carriage Company, Deganwy, 1992

Previous Registrations

GIL2784	F680JKR	RJI2713	G506YFE	A19KFC	G994UKL	
GIL2786	From New	RJI2714	G507YFE	H11KFC	H811HVT, BVA300, H652NFA	
GIL8490	E989KJF	A14KFC	G338KWE	K13KFC	K212SFP	
KIB545	G416WPA	A18KFC	G961UKL			

Livery
Primrose with three tone green relief.
A few vehicles still carry the old livery of primrose with lime green and dark brown relief.

Although The Kings Ferry are better known for their regular daily commuter services into London from the Medway towns, private hires also account for a lot of their commitments. One vehicle which caters for the latter activity is this Toyota Coaster, one of two in the mainly high specification fleet. On a trip to Wembley Stadium in May 1994 is No.2.1. *Colin Lloyd*

It cannot be denied that variety is rife in The Kings Ferry fleet, with almost all new types of bodywork and chassis tested for suitability. Seen turning into Elizabeth Bridge in September 1994 is No.4.6, one of a batch of four Mercedes-Benz 0303 integrals purchased new in 1991 and still looking in excellent condition. *Colin Lloyd*

Since its launch in Britain in 1993, the attractive Irizar Century seems as if it has already outsold all previous Irizar models imported. To date, there is only one in The Kings Ferry fleet. October 1994 finds 4.23 caught up in the usual heavy evening traffic along Victoria Street on its way back to its Kent base. *Colin Lloyd*

Recent developments and vehicle replacements with The Kings Ferry operation have seen the last of the Neoplans replaced by a pair of high specification Berkhof Excellence 2000 HD bodied Scania K113TRAs. The first of the pair is 7.3, here being utilised on commuter route C1 when viewed in Parliament Square in April 1994. *Colin Lloyd*

LACEY'S

Lacey's (East Ham) Ltd, 222 Barking Road, East Ham, London, E6 3BB

✗ RIB1736	Leyland Leopard PSU5C/4R	Plaxton Supreme IV	C53F	1979	
RIB1737	Leyland Leopard PSU5C/4R	Plaxton Supreme IV	C53F	1980	
PRO444W	Volvo B58-61	Plaxton Supreme IV	C34FT	1980	
UHM79	Volvo B10M-61	Plaxton Supreme IV	C53F	1981	
ANK328X	Leyland Tiger TRCTL11/3R	Plaxton Supreme IV	C53F	1982	
A150RMJ	Leyland Tiger TRCTL11/3R	Plaxton Paramount 3500	C55F	1984	Ex Cavalier, Hounslow, 1985
B380AMH	Leyland Royal Tiger B50	Van Hool Alizee H	C49FT	1985	
C901FMP	Leyland Tiger TRCTL11/3RZ	Duple 340	C57F	1986	
D325ACK	Hestair Duple 425 SDA1510	Duple 425	C53F	1987	
E255MMM	Leyland Tiger TRCL10/3ARZA	Van Hool Alizee	C50FT	1988	

Named Vehicle
E255MMM   Lacey's Pullman.

Previous Registrations
RIB1736   GBM113T   RIB1737   MNM39V   UHM79   OLJ193W

Livery
Grey with red relief.

LEOLINE TRAVEL

D.A. Baker, 43 Chiswick Common Road, London, W4 1EZ

✗ GFE622	DAF MB200DKTL600	Jonckheere Bermuda	C53FT	1982	Ex Eagre, Morton, 1992
EOF341	Volvo B10M-61	Jonckheere Jubilee P50	C51FT	1983	Ex Good News Travel, Hull, 1993
IIB8566	Volvo B10M-61	Caetano Algarve	C49FT	1986	Ex Irvine, Law, 1994
F818OJF	Toyota Coaster HB31R	Caetano Optimo	C20F	1988	Ex Link Line, London, NW10, 1994

Previous Registrations
EOF341   UTN940Y, GNT708, LAG236Y   GFE622   WRK30X, LSV112, FTL956X   IIB8566   C676KDS

Livery
White with blue and red, or yellow and green stripes.

LEWIS

Lewis (Greenwich) Ltd, 165 Trafalgar Road, Greenwich, London, SE10 9TX

✗ IIW670	AEC Reliance 6U3ZR	Willowbrook Crusader (1990)	C51F	1973	
IIW6791	AEC Reliance 6U3ZR	Plaxton Supreme III	C51F	1977	Ex RACS, London SE18, 1983
IIW783	AEC Reliance 6U3ZR	Duple Dominant II	C53F	1978	
ONM97V	Volvo B58-61	Plaxton Viewmaster IV	C57F	1979	Ex JPR Coaches, Margate, 1994
IIW628	AEC Reliance 6U3ZR	Van Hool Aragon	C53F	1980	Ex Hookway, Caterham, 1992
UHH267	MAN SR240	MAN	C47FT	1980	Ex Jackson, London E17, 1994
90RYD	Bova FHD12.280	Bova Futura	C49FT	1984	Ex Scotts, London SE14, 1994
A740KFP	Leyland Royal Tiger	Plaxton Paramount 3500	C49FT	1984	Ex Trent Valley Travel, Cannock Wood, 1994
GBZ8302	Volvo B10M-61	Jonckheere Jubilee P599	C51FT	1984	Ex Scotts, London SE14, 1994
IIW372	DAF SB2300DHS585	Jonckheere Jubilee P50	C49FT	1984	Ex Sleight, Swinton, 1993
B138ACK	Leyland Tiger TRCTL11/3RZ	Duple Caribbean 2	C48FT	1985	Ex Sureline, Mayford, 1994
C502AYY	Toyota BB30R	Caetano Optimo	C21F	1986	Ex Martin, Fort Augustus, 1994

Named Vehicles
IIW372   THE CITY CENTRAL PULLMAN   IIW670   MERIDIAN CLIPPER
IIW783   CITY CENTRAL COACH COMPANY

Previous registrations
90RYD	A661EMY	IIW628	NMJ292V	UHH267	GPA609V
GBZ8302	A158PUD	IIW783	YMJ559S	ONM97V	YBK101V, 178DEW
IIW372	A582XRP	IIW6791	UGP98R	A740KFP	A327XHE, HEK965

Livery
White with blue and red relief.
IIW6791 and ONM97V carry BJ Coaches fleetnames.
90RYD and GBZ8302 carry F.Scott & Daughters fleetnames.

Bought new in 1979, RIB1736 is now the oldest vehicle in Lacey's fleet. This 12-metre Leyland Leopard has a Plaxton Supreme IV body and was photographed on a private hire at Chelmsford Bus Station still looking in fine condition. F.Lawrance

LIMEBOURNE

Limebourne Travel Ltd, The BR Depot, Silverthorne Road, London, SW8 3HE

	Reg	Chassis	Body	Seats	Year	Notes
	E309OMG	Volvo B10M-61	Plaxton Paramount 3500 III	C49FT	1988	Ex London Cityrama, London SW8, 1993
	G817YJF	Bova FHG12-290	Bova Futura	C55F	1990	Ex London Cityrama, London SW8, 1993
X	G819YJF	Bova FHD12-290	Bova Futura	C49FT	1990	Ex London Cityrama, London SW8, 1993
	G826YJF	Bova FHD12-290	Bova Futura	C49FT	1990	Ex London Cityrama, London SW8, 1993
	G827YJF	Bova FHD12-290	Bova Futura	C49FT	1990	Ex London Cityrama, London SW8, 1993
	G153XJF	MAN 10-180	Caetano Algarve	C35F	1990	Ex London Cityrama, London SW8, 1993
	J657CYO	Volvo B10M-60	Plaxton Expressliner	C46FT	1991	Ex London Cityrama, London SW8, 1993
X	J213XKY	Scania K113CRB	Plaxton Paramount 3500 III	C51FT	1991	Ex Westerham Coaches, 1993
	J214XKY	Scania K113CRB	Plaxton Paramount 3500 III	C51FT	1991	Ex Westerham Coaches, 1993
	K121CUR	Volvo B10M-60	Plaxton Excalibur 350	C49FT	1993	
	K123CUR	Dennis Javelin 12SDA2117	Plaxton Premiere 320	C57F	1993	
X	L780GMJ	Dennis Javelin 12SDA2117	Plaxton Premiere 320	C57F	1993	
	L982OGY	Bova FLD12-270	Bova Futura	C53F	1994	
	L987OGY	Bova FHD12-340	Bova Futura	C53F	1994	
	L992OGY	Bova FLD12-270	Bova Futura	C53F	1994	
	L993OGY	Bova FLD12-270	Bova Futura	C53F	1994	
	L182PMX	Bova FHD12-340	Bova Futura	C53F	1994	
	L76RAK	Bova FHD12-340	Bova Futura	C51FT	1994	
	L206RAK	Bova FHD12-340	Bova Futura	C53F	1994	
	M259BGF	Bova FLD12-270	Bova Futura	C53F	1994	

Livery
Metallic blue with red and white fleetnames.

Special Liveries
Excalibur Travel (Metallic blue): K121CUR, L780GMJ
National Express Rapide (White with red and blue stripes): J657CYO
Trafalgar Tours (White with rainbow stripes): K123CUR, L982OGY, L987OGY, L992OGY, L993OGY
White Eagle Lines (Pink and white): J213XKY, J214XKY

May 1994 and a rain soaked Buckingham Palace Road welcomes Leoline Travel's GFE622. Among the all-foreign fleet is this mid-engined DAF MB200 carrying a Jonckheere Bermuda body, now a popular choice with many coach companies.
Colin Lloyd

Lewis of Greenwich are one of the oldest London coach operators in existence, dating back to 1919. Not quite that old is this Willowbrook Crusader rebodied AEC Reliance. IIW670 approaches Putney Bridge clearly showing its name, Lewis Meridian Clipper. Van Hool Aragon bodied AEC Reliance IIW628 is unusual in that production of the Reliance ceased soon after the Aragon was introduced onto the UK market. The Aragon was the forerunner to the Alizee range so common today.
Colin Lloyd

One of the few coaches still in the Limebourne standard fleet livery is G819YJF. Most of the newer examples have been delivered in a white base livery and carry insignia for various tour operators. Colin Lloyd

Below **Of the eight Bova Futuras purchased during 1994, five are of the low floor FLD variant although all have the revised front panels incorporating the new indicator assembly. Limebourne's Trafalgar Tours liveried L982OGY was in Parliament Square in June 1994.**
Colin Lloyd

Among a mixed fleet of coaches with Limebourne are a pair of Plaxton Paramount 3500 bodied Scania K113s acquired second hand in 1993. Photographed in Cardiff in February 1994, J213XKY carries the contract livery of White Eagle Lines.
David Donati

Yet another strange vehicle in this publication is the North West Sales Buffalo bodied Mercedes-Benz 814L of Link Line. Retaining the truck style cab rather than the normal coach design, H283HLM lays over in their Wrottlesey Road yard in late 1994.

LINK LINE PULLMAN

Clay Lake Travel Ltd, 1 Wrottesley Road, London, NW10 5XA

C493TBC	Ford Transit 190D	Alexander	B16F	1985	Ex Midland Fox, 1994	
C501TJF	Ford Transit 190D	Alexander	C12F	1985	Ex Horsham Coaches, 1994	
F768XNH	LAG Panoramic	LAG	C51FT	1989		
G841VAY	Mercedes-Benz 609D	Reeve Burgess Beaver	C23F	1989		
G474XLF	Mercedes-Benz 609D	Mellor	C19F	1989	Ex Amanda, Bedfont, 1994	
G118CLD	Mercedes-Benz 811D	Optare StarRider	C29F	1990	Ex Wings, Uxbridge, 1994	
G119CLD	Mercedes-Benz 811D	Optare StarRider	C29F	1990	Ex Wings, Uxbridge, 1994	
X H283HLM	Mercedes-Benz 814D	North West Buffalo	C35F	1991		
H123WFM	Mercedes-Benz 814D	North West	C24F	1991		

Previous Registrations
G118CLD   G839LWR, WLT732
G119CLD   G383ALM, WLT852

Livery
Red, fawn and gold.

THE LONDONERS

The Londoners Ltd, 1a Bradbourne Grove, London, SE15 2BS

The Londoners Tacho Centre Ltd, 1a Bradbourne Grove, London, SE15 2BS

T	E219GNV	Volvo B10M-61	Jonckheere Jubilee P599	C51FT	1987	
X	E691NNH	Volvo B10M-61	Jonckheere Jubilee P50	C51FT	1988	
	E692NNH	Volvo B10M-61	Jonckheere Jubilee P599	C51FT	1988	
	E693NNH	Volvo B10M-61	Jonckheere Jubilee P599	C51FT	1988	
	E694NNH	Volvo B10M-61	Jonckheere Jubilee P599	C51FT	1988	
T	F414DUG	Volvo B10M-60	Plaxton Paramount 3500 III	C50F	1989	Ex Wallace Arnold, Leeds, 1994
	F418DUG	Volvo B10M-60	Plaxton Paramount 3500 III	C50F	1989	Ex Jones, Llandeilo, 1994
	F419DUG	Volvo B10M-60	Plaxton Paramount 3500 III	C50F	1989	Ex Wallace Arnold, Leeds, 1994
	F695PAY	Hestair Duple 425 SDA1510	Duple 425	C57F	1989	
	F696PAY	Hestair Duple 425 SDA1510	Duple 425	C57F	1989	
	G546NKJ	Volvo B10M-60	Caetano Algarve	C53F	1989	Ex The Kings Ferry, Gillingham, 1993
	G998RKN	Volvo B10M-60	Caetano Algarve	C49FT	1990	Ex The Kings Ferry, Gillingham, 1993
T	H182EJF	Toyota Coaster HB31R	Caetano Optimo II	C18F	1991	
	J96UBL	Dennis Javelin 12SDA2101	Berkhof Excellence 2000	C53F	1992	
	J97UBL	Dennis Javelin 12SDA2101	Berkhof Excellence 2000	C53F	1992	
	J98UBL	Dennis Javelin 12SDA2101	Berkhof Excellence 2000	C53F	1992	
TX	M725LYP	Dennis Javelin 12SDA2131	Plaxton Premiere 320 II	C53F	1994	

T - Denotes vehicles in the Londoners Tacho Centre fleet.

Livery
Magenta and white with pink relief.
F418DUG is white and carries Kuoni fleetnames.
Two tone blue and white: E691NNH

LONDON COACHES / NORTH KENT ROADCAR (Pullmans Group Limited)

London Coaches Ltd, Jews Row, Wandsworth, London, SW18 1TB
North Kent Roadcar Company Ltd, Lower Road, Northfleet, Kent, DA11 9SN

Joint coach fleet

DS3	KJF300V	Volvo B58-56	Duple Dominant II	C53F	1980	Ex London Buses, 1992
DV11	F611HGO	DAF SB3000DKV601	Van Hool Alizee SH	C53F	1989	Ex London Buses, 1992
DV12	F612HGO	DAF SB3000DKV601	Van Hool Alizee SH	C53F	1989	Ex London Buses, 1992
DV16	F616HGO	DAF SB2305DHS585	Van Hool Alizee H	C53F	1989	Ex London Buses, 1992
DV17	F617HGO	DAF SB2305DHS585	Van Hool Alizee H	C53F	1989	Ex London Buses, 1992
DV18	F618HGO	DAF MB230LT615	Van Hool Alizee SH	C53FT	1989	Ex London Buses, 1992
DV19	F619HGO	DAF MB230LB615	Van Hool Alizee SH	C53FT	1989	Ex London Buses, 1992
DV20	F620HGO	DAF MB230LB615	Van Hool Alizee SH	C52FT	1989	Ex London Buses, 1992
DV21	F621HGO	DAF MB230LT615	Van Hool Alizee SH	C53FT	1989	Ex London Buses, 1992
DV22	F622HGO	DAF MB230LT615	Van Hool Alizee SH	C52FT	1989	Ex London Buses, 1992
DV23	H523YCX	DAF SB2305DHS585	Van Hool Alizee H	C53F	1991	Ex London Buses, 1992
DV24	H524YCX	DAF SB2305DHS585	Van Hool Alizee H	C53F	1991	Ex London Buses, 1992
DV26	H526YCX	DAF SB2305DHS585	Van Hool Alizee H	C53F	1991	Ex London Buses, 1992
DV27	H527YCX	DAF SB2305DHS585	Van Hool Alizee H	C53F	1991	Ex London Buses, 1992
DV29	H529YCX	DAF SB2305DHS585	Van Hool Alizee H	C53F	1991	Ex London Buses, 1992
DV31	H531YCX	DAF SB2305DHS585	Van Hool Alizee H	C53F	1991	Ex London Buses, 1992
DV32	J432NCP	DAF SB2305DHS585	Van Hool Alizee H	C53F	1992	Ex London Buses, 1992
DV33	J433NCP	DAF SB2305DHS585	Van Hool Alizee H	C53F	1992	Ex London Buses, 1992
DV34	J434NCP	DAF SB2305DHS585	Van Hool Alizee H	C53F	1992	Ex London Buses, 1992
DV35	J435NCP	DAF SB2305DHS585	Van Hool Alizee H	C53F	1992	Ex London Buses, 1992
DV42	K542RJX	DAF SB3000DKV601	Van Hool Alizee HE	C53F	1993	
DV43	K543RJX	DAF SB3000DKV601	Van Hool Alizee HE	C53F	1993	
DV44	K544RJX	DAF SB3000DKV601	Van Hool Alizee HE	C53F	1993	
DV48	L548EHD	DAF SB3000DKVF601	Van Hool Alizee HE	C55F	1993	
DV49	L549EHD	DAF SB3000DKVF601	Van Hool Alizee HE	C55F	1993	
DV50	L550EHD	DAF SB3000DKVF601	Van Hool Alizee HE	C55F	1993	
DV51	L551EHD	DAF SB3000DKVF601	Van Hool Alizee HE	C55F	1993	
DV52	L552EHD	DAF SB3000DKVF601	Van Hool Alizee HE	C55F	1993	
DV53	L553EHD	DAF SB3000DKVF601	Van Hool Alizee HE	C55F	1993	
DV54	L554EHD	DAF SB3000DKVF601	Van Hool Alizee HE	C55F	1993	
DV59	F259RJX	DAF SB3000DKV601	Van Hool Alizee H	C53F	1989	Ex London Buses, 1992
DV60	F260RJX	DAF SB3000DKV601	Van Hool Alizee H	C53F	1989	Ex London Buses, 1992
DV62	G962KJX	DAF SB2305DHS585	Van Hool Alizee H	C53F	1990	Ex London Buses, 1992
DV63	G963KJX	DAF SB2305DHS585	Van Hool Alizee H	C53F	1990	Ex London Buses, 1992
DV64	G964KJX	DAF SB3000DKV601	Van Hool Alizee H	C53F	1990	Ex London Buses, 1992
DV65	G965KJX	DAF SB3000DKV585	Van Hool Alizee H	C53F	1990	Ex London Buses, 1992
DV66	G966KJX	DAF SB3000DKV601	Van Hool Alizee H	C53F	1990	Ex London Buses, 1992
DV71	M571RCP	DAF SB3000WS601	Van Hool Alizee HE	C55F	1994	
DV72	M572RCP	DAF SB3000WS601	Van Hool Alizee HE	C55F	1994	
DV73	M573RCP	DAF SB3000WS601	Van Hool Alizee HE	C55F	1994	
DV74	M574RCP	DAF SB3000WS601	Van Hool Alizee HE	C55F	1994	
DV75	M575RCP	DAF SB3000WS601	Van Hool Alizee HE	C55F	1994	
DV76	M576RCP	DAF SB3000WS601	Van Hool Alizee HE	C55F	1994	
DV77	M577RCP	DAF SB3000WS601	Van Hool Alizee HE	C55F	1994	
DV78	M578RCP	DAF SB3000WS601	Van Hool Alizee HE	C55F	1994	
DV79	M579RCP	DAF SB3000WS601	Van Hool Alizee HE	C55F	1994	
DV80	M580RCP	DAF SB3000WS601	Van Hool Alizee HE	C55F	1994	
DV84	J784KHD	DAF SB3000DKV601	Van Hool Alizee H	C53F	1992	Ex Hughes-DAF, Gomershal, 1994
DV85	J785KHD	DAF SB3000DKV601	Van Hool Alizee H	C53F	1992	Ex Hughes-DAF, Gomershal, 1994
DV112	K512RJX	DAF SB3000DKV601	Van Hool Alizee H	C53F	1994	
DV113	K513RJX	DAF SB3000DKV601	Van Hool Alizee H	C53F	1994	
DV114	K514RJX	DAF SB3000DKV601	Van Hool Alizee H	C53F	1994	

Livery
Red with gold fleetnames.
Most of the fleet still carry London Coaches fleetnames, but those operated by North Kent Roadcar were beginning to acquire their new Company logos at the time of going to press.

Operations
London Coaches: DV18-21, 59, 60/4-6
North Kent Roadcar: DV11/2/6/7, 22-24/6/7/9, 31-35, 42-4/8-54, 62/3, 71-80/4/5, 112-4, DD1-4.
Driver Training: DS3

The Londoners have a quintet of Jonckheere Jubilees, all based on the Volvo B10M chassis. The odd one out is E691NNH, the sole P50 type and also the only one to carry the white and two tone blue livery. The National Gallery in Trafalgar Square provides the background. David Savage

The latest vehicle to join The Londoners is this Plaxton Premiere 320 II bodied Dennis Javelin. A very sunny 1st November finds M725LYP crossing the yet to be rebuilt Kingston Bridge. Geoff Rixon

Great Smith Street, Westminster sees London Coaches DV 22 in July 1994 about to begin its trip on commuter route W back to Kent. The London Coaches fleet consists entirely of DAF/Van Hools and they are possibly the largest user of the type in Britain. Colin Lloyd

London Coaches DV 76 was one of the ten new Van Hool bodied DAFs to join the fleet in 1994. August finds the coach parked on the Embankment a few weeks before becoming the first vehicle in the fleet to have North Kent fleetnames applied. Colin Lloyd

MARSHALLS

F.W. Marshall, 16 North Street, Leighton Buzzard, Bucks, LU7 9EN

Reg	Chassis	Body	Seating	Year	Notes
848FXN	Volvo B58-61	Plaxton Supreme IV	C53F	1979	Ex Poulson, Copford, 1987
JDB949V	Ford R1114	Plaxton Supreme IV	C49F	1980	Ex Transauto, Chesham, 1993
GSU384	Volvo B58-61	Jonckheere Bermuda	C53F	1981	Ex Transauto, Chesham, 1993
1404FM	Volvo B10M-61	Jonckheere Bermuda	C40FT	1981	Ex Trathens, Roborough, 1983
FSU379	Auwaerter Neoplan N122/3	Auwaerter Skyliner	CH56/20CT	1982	Ex Ebdons, Sidcup, 1994
SM9562	Scania K112CRS	Jonckheere Jubilee P599	C51F	1984	
MJI6253	Scania K112CRS	Jonckheere Jubilee P599	C53F	1985	
B39KAL	Volvo B10M-61	Jonckheere Jubilee P50	C53F	1985	Ex Jetsie, Hoddesdon, 1991
B43KAL	Volvo B10M-61	Jonckheere Jubilee P50	C53F	1985	Ex Skills, Nottingham, 1992
B794EGG	Volvo B10M-61	Jonckheere Jubilee P50	C53F	1985	Ex Collison, Stonehouse, 1992
B891MAB	Bedford YNT	Duple Laser	C53F	1985	Ex Ronsway, Hemel Hempstead, 1994
MIJ3409	Volvo B10M-53	Jonckheere Jubilee P95	CH54/13DT	1985	Ex Happy Al's, Birkenhead, 1993
C951GWO	Scania K112CRS	Jonckheere Jubilee P599	C57F	1985	Ex Transauto, Chesham, 1993
MJI6252	Volvo B10M-61	Jonckheere Jubilee P50	C51FT	1986	
D208VEV	Volvo B10M-61	Berkhof Esprite 350	C53F	1987	Ex Transauto, Chesham, 1993
D508WNV	Bedford Venturer YNV	Caetano Algarve	C57F	1987	Ex Ronsway, Hemel Hempstead, 1994
E700GNH	Iveco 315.8.17	Caetano Algarve	C28F	1987	Ex Scancoaches, London NW10, 1994
E39LNH	MAN MT8.136	Reeve Burgess Riviera	C32F	1988	Ex Country Lion, Northampton, 1994
E753YKU	Volvo B10M-61	Plaxton Paramount 3500 III	C53F	1988	Ex Transauto, Chesham, 1993
E754YKU	Volvo B10M-61	Plaxton Paramount 3500 III	C53F	1988	Ex Transauto, Chesham, 1993
G166RBD	Volvo B10M-60	Jonckheere Deauville P599	C34FT	1990	
H607SWG	Volvo B10M-60	Ikarus Blue Danube 336	C53F	1990	
H608SWG	Volvo B10M-60	Ikarus Blue Danube 336	C53F	1990	
L110RWB	Volvo B10M-60	Plaxton Excalibur	C53F	1994	
M250TAK	Scania K113CRB	Irizar Century	C49F	1994	

Previous Registrations

1404FM	XNV150W	GSU384	XNV138W	MJI6253	B500GBD
848FXN	BHX850T	MIJ3409	B705EOF	B794EGG	B40KAL, UBM880
SM9562	A112SNH	MJI6252	C414LRP	B891MAB	LSV548
FSU379	GVL939Y		C951GWO	B68MLT	

Livery
Blue with red, orange and yellow stripes.
Newbourne Coaches (White with red, yellow and blue relief): GSU384, C951GWO, D208VEV, E753YKU, E754YKU
Ronsway fleetnames: FSU379, MJI6253, B891MAB, D508WNV.

METROBUS

Metrobus Ltd, Farnborough Hill, Orpington, Kent, BR6 6DA

Reg	Chassis	Body	Seating	Year	Notes
ODV405W	AEC Reliance 6U2R	Duple Dominant II Express	C53F	1981	Ex Tillingbourne, Cranleigh, 1983
B688BPU	Leyland Olympian ONTL11/2Rsp	Eastern Coach Works	CH45/28F	1985	Ex Thamesway, 1991
E597LVH	DAF MB2300DKVL615	Duple 320	C57F	1988	Ex KF Cars, Gatwick, 1991
E957GGX	DAF MB2300DKVL615	Duple 320	C57F	1988	
G426YAY	Dennis Javelin 12SDA1907	Duple 320	C53FT	1990	Ex Jason's, Swanley, 1993
G427YAY	Dennis Javelin 12SDA1907	Duple 320	C53FT	1990	Ex Jason's, Swanley, 1993
G428YAY	Dennis Javelin 12SDA1907	Duple 320	C53FT	1990	Ex Jason's, Swanley, 1993
G429YAY	Dennis Javelin 12SDA1907	Duple 320	C53FT	1990	Ex Jason's, Swanley, 1993
H220JLJ	Leyland Tiger TRCL10/3ARZA	Plaxton 321	C57F	1990	
J201FMX	Leyland Tiger TRCL10/3ARZM	Plaxton 321	C53F	1991	
J202FMX	Leyland Tiger TRCL10/3ARZM	Plaxton 321	C53F	1991	
J51SNY	Leyland Tiger TRCL10/3ARZM	Plaxton 321	C53F	1991	Ex Bebb, Llantwit Fardre, 1992
J52SNY	Leyland Tiger TRCL10/3ARZM	Plaxton 321	C53F	1991	Ex Bebb, Llantwit Fardre, 1992
J577PNK	Ford Transit	Ford	C11F	1992	Ex Bicknell's, Godalming, 1994
K203GMX	Dennis Javelin 12SDA2117	Plaxton Premiere 320	C49FT	1993	
K204GMX	Dennis Javelin 12SDA2117	Plaxton Premiere 320	C49FT	1993	
K205GMX	Dennis Javelin 12SDA2117	Plaxton Premiere 320	C49FT	1993	
K206GMX	Dennis Javelin 12SDA2117	Plaxton Premiere 320	C49FT	1993	
L207PGU	Mercedes-Benz 709D	Plaxton Beaver	C25F	1994	
M208BGK	Dennis Javelin 12SDA2131	Plaxton Premiere 320 II	C53F	1994	
M209BGK	Dennis Javelin 12SDA2131	Plaxton Premiere 320 II	C53F	1994	

Named Vehicle
J577PNK Metrobus Mini Cruiser

Livery
Blue, white and yellow.
J201FMX and J202FMX carry Southlands fleetnames.

Special liveries
Hoverspeed City Sprint (White with red and blue relief): G428 YAY, K203-206 GMX

MITCHAM BELLE COACHES

Wimco Group (Coaches) Ltd, 223 Streatham Road, Mitcham, Surrey, CR4 2AJ

NUR91P	Bedford YLQ	Plaxton Supreme III	C45F	1976	Ex Hall, London SW16, 1988
RHV990R	Leyland Leopard PSU3C/4R	Plaxton Supreme III	C53F	1977	Ex Lewis, Carshalton, 1992
BGY591T	Leyland Leopard PSU5C/4R	Plaxton Supreme IV	C50F	1979	Ex National Travel London, 1983
XHT26T	Bedford YMT	Plaxton Supreme IV	C53F	1979	Ex Baker's, Weston-super-Mare, 1992
EPM143V	AEC Reliance 6U2R	Plaxton Supreme IV Express	C53F	1979	Ex Harding, Betchworth, 1991
EPM145V	AEC Reliance 6U2R	Plaxton Supreme IV Express	C53F	1979	Ex Harding, Betchworth, 1990
C116AFX	Bedford Venturer YNV	Plaxton Paramount 3200 II	C53F	1986	Ex Wright, Worthing, 1994
E636AWB	Ford Transit	Ford	M11	1988	Ex private owner, 1992
E846PPR	Ford Transit	Ford	M14	1989	Ex Tern Rent-a-Car, Norwich, 1991
F480KBD	Mercedes-Benz 609D	Made To Measure	C24F	1989	Ex Online, Sutton, 1993
JSK957	Dennis Javelin 12SDA1907	Duple 320	C53F	1989	Ex Maybury, Cranborne, 1993
JSK958	Dennis Javelin 12SDA1907	Duple 320	C53F	1989	Ex Maybury, Cranborne, 1993
F578VRU	Ford Transit	Ford	M11	1989	Ex private owner, 1992
F50YEL	Ford Transit	Ford	M14	1989	
F51YEL	Ford Transit	Ford	M14	1989	
F52YEL	Ford Transit	Ford	M14	1989	
F53YEL	Ford Transit	Ford	M14	1989	
F54YEL	Ford Transit	Ford	M14	1989	
H755FLL	Ford Transit	Ford	M11	1990	Ex London Borough of Merton, 1992
J28RFD	DAF 400	Jubilee (1994)	C16F	1992	Ex private owner, 1994
K755SWD	Leyland-DAF 400	Jubilee	C16F	1992	

Livery
White or silver with orange, blue and grey relief.

Previous Registrations
XHT26T   DYA978T, 7636LJ   JSK957   F492WPR   JSK958   F239OFP

NAUGHTON'S

Naughton Minicoach Services Ltd, 52 Walsingham Gardens, Stoneleigh, Surrey, KT19 0LU

XLN588X	Ford R1114	Duple Dominant IV	C53F	1982	
PDT825X	Ford R1114	Plaxton Supreme V	C53F	1982	Ex Bowers, Chapel-en-le-Frith, 1985
F630SAY	Dennis Javelin 11SDL1905	Duple 320	C55F	1989	

Livery
White and blue

NEW BHARAT COACHES

New Bharat Coaches Ltd, 1 Priory Way, Southall, Middx, UB2 5HN

TNP615Y	Volvo B10M-61	Duple Laser	C57F	1983	Ex AMS, Maidenhead, 1994
PJI1823	Volvo B10M-61	Plaxton Paramount 3500	C52FT	1983	
D254HFX	Volvo B10M-61	Plaxton Paramount 3200 III	C53F	1987	Ex Pathfinder, Chadwell Heath, 1992
PJI1824	Volvo B10M-61	Plaxton Paramount 3200 III	C53F	1987	Ex Shearings, Wigan, 1992
E597UHS	Volvo B10M-61	Plaxton Paramount 3500 III	C53F	1988	Ex Barratt, Nantwich, 1994
F661LAR	Volvo B10M-61	Plaxton Paramount 3500 III	C49FT	1988	Ex Brandon, Blackmore End, 1993
F214NLE	Volvo B10M-61	Plaxton Paramount 3500 III	C53FT	1988	
F104CCL	Volvo B10M-61	Plaxton Paramount 3500 III	C53F	1989	Ex Travellers, Hounslow, 1993

Previous Registrations
PJI1823   A849EAY   PJI1824   D570MVR, ESU117, D464GEN

Livery
Cream and yellow.

Marshalls of Leighton Buzzard's low height Ikarus Blue Danube was taking a break between commuter service runs in November 1994. H607SWG is one of a pair bought new in 1990 and is seen parked opposite the Tate Gallery in Millbank. Colin Lloyd

Acquired by Marshalls in 1993, Newbourne Coaches still retain their former livery as depicted here by D208VEV. Although the Volvo B10M is a popular choice within the fleet, this Esprite is the solitary Berkhof bodied example. The coach is approaching journey's end, turning into Eccleston Street, Victoria. Colin Lloyd

Metrobus of Orpington number among the few companies to have bought the short lived Plaxton 321; three from new and two second hand examples are in stock. The 321 was a Plaxton built version of the Duple 320 although few were built. J201FMX represents one of those bought new, seen in Loam Pit Vale, Lewisham having had Southlands fleetnames added since the acquisition of this company in 1991. Keith Grimes

With the acquisition of Jasons Coaches of Swanley in 1993 came the takeover of the Hoverspeed contract. Four new Dennis Javelins with Plaxton Premiere bodies were purchased for this contract and all carry this dedicated livery. Leaving Victoria Coach Station when new in September 1993 is K206GMX.
Colin Lloyd

As well as private hires, Mitcham Belle also cater for school contracts and, as shown here by former Green Line EPM145V, mystery tours. Hampton Court Way, Thames Ditton in November 1994 finds this excellent example of an AEC Reliance deceptive of its 1979 vintage.
Geoff Rixon

Putney High Street in April 1994 provides the setting for Naughton's F630SAY, the only Dennis Javelin in the otherwise Bedford fleet.
Colin Lloyd

83

The oldest vehicle owned by New Bharat of Southall is this Volvo B10M with Duple Laser body. Until recently, the company had a pair of Volvo C10M coaches, but alas they have now gone. Seen in the depot yard in a dreary October 1994 is TNP615Y.
Keith Grimes

PEMICO TRAVEL

R.G. Sault & E.R. Roff, 9-11 Verney Road, London, SE16 3DH

ABE543W	Mercedes-Benz L207D	Devon Conversions	M12	1980	Ex Hatfield, Beckenham, 1985
KGT459Y	Mercedes-Benz L207D	Devon Conversions	M12	1982	Ex Film Service, London NW10, 1986
A324EGX	Ford Transit	Trimoco	M12	1983	
A942UCY	Bedford VAS5	Wadham Stringer Vangaurd	DP23FL	1984	Ex West Glamorgan County Council, 1989
A949UCY	Bedford VAS5	Wadham Stringer Vangaurd	DP23FL	1984	Ex West Glamorgan County Council, 1989
FIL4138	Bedford YMP	Plaxton Paramount 3200 II	C28F	1985	Ex Armchair, Brentford, 1990
FIL4139	Bedford YMP	Plaxton Paramount 3200 II	C28F	1985	Ex Armchair, Brentford, 1990
IIL2496	Leyland Tiger TRCTL11/3RZ	Plaxton Paramount 3500 III	C53F	1987	
IIL2497	Leyland Tiger TRCTL11/3RZ	Plaxton Paramount 3500 III	C49FT	1987	
E971SVU	Mercedes-Benz 307D	Made To Measure	M12	1987	
E972SVU	Mercedes-Benz 307D	Made To Measure	M12	1987	
E973SVU	Mercedes-Benz 307D	Made To Measure	M12	1987	
E829PJT	Ford Transit	Ford	M11	1988	Ex private owner, 1994
IIL2476	Leyland Tiger TRCTL11/3RZ	Plaxton Paramount 3200 III	C53F	1988	Ex Shearings, Wigan, 1992
IIL2487	Leyland Tiger TRCTL11/3RZ	Plaxton Paramount 3200 III	C53F	1988	Ex Shearings, Wigan, 1992
F871RFP	Dennis Javelin 12SDA1907	Duple 320	C53F	1989	
F872RFP	Dennis Javelin 12SDA1907	Duple 320	C53F	1989	
F873RFP	Dennis Javelin 12SDA1907	Duple 320	C53F	1989	
F874RFP	Dennis Javelin 12SDA1907	Duple 320	C53F	1989	
F875RFP	Dennis Javelin 12SDA1907	Duple 320	C53F	1989	
G508JHB	Mercedes-Benz 408D	Devon Conversions	C16F	1990	Ex Inter-European Airways, Cardiff, 1994
J218XKY	Scania K93CRB	Van Hool Alizee H	C55F	1992	
J219XKY	Scania K93CRB	Van Hool Alizee H	C55F	1992	
J220XKY	Scania K93CRB	Van Hool Alizee H	C55F	1992	
L146OUM	Mercedes-Benz 609D	Autobus Classique	C23F	1994	
M351TDO	Mercedes-Benz 814D	Autobus Classique	C33F	1994	
M352TDO	Mercedes-Benz 814D	Autobus Classique	C33F	1994	

Previous Registrations
FIL4138	B409CMC	IIL2476	E681UNE	IIL2496	E964NMK
FIL4139	B410CMC	IIL2487	E686UNE	IIL2497	E965NMK

Livery
White.

PRAIRIE

Prairie Coaches Ltd, Unit 3 Green Lane, Hounslow, Middx, TW4 6BY

EAC876T	Bedford YMT	Plaxton Supreme IV Express	C53F	1979	Ex Shoestock, Ickenham, 1990
FDU806T	Bedford YMT	Plaxton Supreme IV Express	C53F	1979	Ex Shoestock, Ickenham, 1990
FKX285T	Bedford YMT	Duple Dominant II	C53F	1979	
848KMX	Volvo B10M-61	Jonckheere Jubilee P50	C48DT	1983	Ex Travellers, Hounslow, 1991
315ASV	Volvo B10M-61	Jonckheere Jubilee P50	C48DT	1983	Ex Travellers, Hounslow, 1991
A186MNE	Volvo B10M-61	Van Hool Alizee H	C49FT	1984	Ex Moon, Horsham, 1992
PIJ411	Volvo B10M-61	Berkhof Esprite 340	C53F	1984	Ex The Kings Ferry, Gillingham, 1989
165RPH	Volvo B10M-61	Berkhof Esprite 340	C53F	1984	Ex The Kings Ferry, Gillingham, 1989
SIJ701	Volvo B10M-61	Plaxton Paramount 3200 II	C43F	1985	Ex Capital, West Drayton, 1991
FIL7665	Bova FHD12-280	Bova Futura	C49FT	1986	Ex Collier, Earith, 1993
E614GMX	LAG Panoramic	LAG	C49FT	1987	Ex Chisholm, Swanley, 1994
CCC257	Volvo B10M-61	Ikarus Blue Danube 336	C49FT	1989	Ex Sutherland, Edinburgh, 1994
SRP209	Volvo B10M-61	Ikarus Blue Danube 336	C53F	1989	Ex Sutherland, Edinburgh, 1994

Previous Registrations

165RPH	A579RVW, LIJ749, A634SKK		CCC257	F109SSE	SIJ701	C160TLF
315ASV	ONV643Y		FIL7665	C972TPV	SRP209	F110SSE
848KMX	ONV641Y		PIJ411	A575RVW, 327WTF, A633SKK	E614GMX	SIB144

Livery
White and turquoise with yellow signwriting.

PREMIER-ALBANIAN

Premier Coaches (Watford) Ltd, 105-107 Queens Avenue, Watford, WD1 7NU

ENT778	Leyland Tiger PS1	Burlingham	C33F	1948	Ex Combs, Ixworth, 1972
LTA904	Bedford OB	Duple Vista	C27F	1949	Ex Rover Bus, Chesham, 1988
LGV994	Bedford SB3	Duple Vega	C41F	1958	Ex Wents, Boxted, 1982
CBM12X	Leyland Tiger TRCTL11/3R	Plaxton Supreme VI	C53F	1982	
CBM13X	Leyland Tiger TRCTL11/3R	Plaxton Supreme VI	C53F	1982	
B21XKX	Leyland Tiger TRCTL11/3R	Plaxton Paramount 3200	C57F	1985	
B22XKX	Leyland Tiger TRCTL11/3R	Plaxton Paramount 3200	C57F	1985	
C24GKX	Iveco 79.14	Caetano Viana	C19F	1986	

ENT778 is in the Associated J.E.Hewitt fleet and carries Premier Omnibus livery.
LGV994 is awaiting restoration.

Livery
Red and cream.

P & S TRAVEL

S.E. Thompson, 91 Cowley Road, Uxbridge, Middx, UB8 2AG

YNN33Y	Volvo B10M-61	LAG Galaxy	C53F	1983	Ex Skill's, Nottingham, 1988
A321LLH	Mercedes-Benz L608D	Reeve Burgess	C19F	1984	
B287AMG	Mercedes-Benz L608D	Reeve Burgess	C25F	1985	
MHU48	Volvo B10M-61	Caetano Algarve	C53F	1985	Ex Pugh, Winterbourne, 1988
C282GMA	Mercedes-Benz L608D	PMT Hanbridge	C24F	1985	Ex Taylor, Tylers Green, 1988
F936SLD	Leyland-DAF 400	Howells	C16F	1989	Ex Lewis, Ipswich, 1994
HIL5681	Sanos S315.21	FAP Charisma	C53F	1989	Ex Chartercoach, Dovercourt, 1994
G821UMU	Leyland Swift LBM6T/2RS	Reeve Burgess Harrier	C37F	1989	
H488BND	Mercedes-Benz 609D	Made To Measure	C26F	1990	
H489BND	Leyland-DAF 400	Made To Measure	C16F	1990	
M325TDO	Mercedes-Benz 814D	Autobus Classique	C33F	1994	

Named Vehicle
MHU48   Silver Dreamliner

Previous Registrations

MHU48	B721MBC	HIL5681	F751SPU

Livery
White with turquoise relief.

Turning into Whitehall in April 1994 is Pemico Travel's J219XKY, a Van Hool Alizee bodied Scania K93CRB. It is one of three bought new in 1992 which remain the newest full-sized vehicles in the fleet. Colin Lloyd

Prairie of Hounslow own this attractive low-height version of the Ikarus Blue Danube with Volvo B10M chassis. It is July 1994 at Hampton Court and the day trippers disembark for a walk round the famous Palace and Gardens. Geoff Rixon

One of several vintage coaches restored to full regular PCV use is Premier-Albanian's superb Leyland Tiger PS1 with Burlingham coachwork. Also in this remarkable fleet is a Bedford OB with Duple Vista body whilst a Bedford SB3 with Duple Vega bodywork is the next one to feel the restorers expert hands. Colin Lloyd

The modest garage in Queens Avenue, Watford provides the setting for CBM13X, a Plaxton Supreme VI bodied Leyland Tiger now in its twelfth year with Premier-Albanian. It was never the most popular choice in the Supreme range of bodywork, most operators preferring the Mk IV or V to the VI.
Keith Grimes

This high-floor, yet low driving position, Caetano Algarve mounted on the ever popular Volvo B10M belongs to P & S Travel of Uxbridge. Named Silver Dreamliner, MHU48 has a crew compartment just ahead of the rear axle. Marble Arch is the location in August 1994.
Colin Lloyd

PROVENCE PRIVATE HIRE

Provence Private Hire Ltd, Heath Farm Lane, Harpenden Road, St Albans, Herts, AL3 5AE

PMR361M	Bedford YRT	Plaxton Panorama Elite III Exp	C53F	1974	Ex H & F Hire, St.Albans, 1993
KFO572P	Bedford VAS5	Plaxton Supreme III	C28FL	1975	Ex Brown, Builth Wells, 1991
PNN427R	Bedford YNT	Plaxton Supreme III	C53F	1976	Ex Mayne, Astley, 1990
XTM482S	Bedford YNT	Plaxton Supreme III	C53F	1978	Ex H & F Hire, St.Albans, 1989
AWB818T	Bedford YMT	Duple Dominant II	C53F	1979	Ex Prestige Furniture, Radlett, 1987
FKX279T	Bristol LHL6L	Plaxton Supreme III	C53F	1979	Ex Mancini, Faversham, 1992
MUE314V	Volvo B58-61	Duple Dominant II	C57F	1980	
FRM688V	Volvo B58-61	Unicar BD57	C57F	1980	Ex Gordon, Kirkbride, 1984
CPP45X	Volvo B10M-61	Duple Dominant III	C53F	1982	
LTY556X	Bedford YNT	Plaxton Supreme VI	C53F	1982	Ex Wilde, Clowne, 1990
SUK431Y	Ford R1115	Duple Dominant IV	C53F	1982	Ex Meadway, Birmingham, 1991
153XYC	Auwaerter Neoplan N112/3	Auwaerter Skyliner	CH53/20CT1982		Ex H & F Hire, St.Albans, 1993
485SWL	Auwaerter Neoplan N112/3	Auwaerter Skyliner	CH53/20CT1983		Ex Reilly, Maghull, 1993
CVH733Y	Ford R1114	Duple Dominant IV	C35F	1983	Ex H & F Hire, St.Albans, 1992
WSU448	MCW Metroliner CR126/8	MCW	C51F	1984	Ex East Kent, 1994
WSU453	MCW Metroliner CR126/8	MCW	C51F	1984	Ex East Kent, 1994
XMW285	MCW Metroliner CR126/8	MCW	C51F	1984	Ex East Kent, 1994
LDZ3144	MCW Metroliner HR131/6	MCW	C49FT	1985	Ex East Kent, 1994
C131CFB	MCW Metroliner HR131/7	MCW	C55F	1986	Ex Wessex, Bristol, 1993
C759CWX	MCW Metroliner DR130/26	MCW	CH57/22FT	1986	Ex Amberline, Speke, 1990
E426ATT	Fiat Ducato	Devon Conversions	M14	1988	Ex London Unit, Swanley, 1992
F862TNH	Volvo B10M-61	Caetano Algarve	C53F	1988	

Previous Registrations

LDZ3144	B244JVA			WSU448	A848OKK	XMW285	A849OKK
485SWL	MVL607Y, 4585SC			WSU453	B853TKL	153XYC	ADV160Y

Livery
Yellow.

R & I COACHES

R & I Tours Ltd, Western Road, Park Royal, London, NW10 7LA

043	C842KGK	Iveco 35.8	Elme		C16F	1985	Ex Limebourne, SW8, 1987
044	C843KGK	Iveco 35.8	Elme		C16F	1985	Ex Limebourne, SW8, 1987
057	E780MLB	Iveco 35.8	Devon Conversions		C12F	1988	Ex Monk, NW10, 1989
058	E783MLB	Iveco 35.8	Devon Conversions		C12F	1988	Ex Monk, NW10, 1989
059	RIB7002	Bedford YMP	Plaxton Supreme V		C35F	1982	Ex Ardenvale, Knowle, 1988
060	E781MLB	Toyota Coaster HB31R	Caetano Optimo		C16F	1988	Ex Monk, NW10, 1989
061	E782MLB	Toyota Coaster HB31R	Caetano Optimo		C21F	1988	Ex Monk, NW10, 1989
064	E784MLB	Toyota Coaster HB31R	Caetano Optimo		C16F	1988	Ex Monk, NW10, 1989
065	E785MLB	Toyota Coaster HB31R	Caetano Optimo		C21F	1988	Ex Monk, NW10, 1989
067	ULL897	Mercedes-Benz 811D	Optare StarRider		C29F	1988	Ex Monk, NW10, 1989
077	C945FMJ	Ford Transit 190D	Chassis Developments		M8	1985	Ex Monk, NW10, 1989
081	RIB6197	Kassbohrer Setra S210HI	Kassbohrer Optimal		C26FT	1989	
082	RIB6198	Kassbohrer Setra S210HI	Kassbohrer Optimal		C26FT	1989	
083	RIB6199	Kassbohrer Setra S210HI	Kassbohrer Optimal		C26FT	1989	
084	F84GGC	Mercedes-Benz 811D	Robin Hood		C29F	1989	
085	F85GGC	Mercedes-Benz 811D	Robin Hood		C29F	1989	
086	F86GGC	Mercedes-Benz 811D	Robin Hood		C29F	1989	
087	F87GGC	Mercedes-Benz 811D	Robin Hood		C29F	1989	
088	F88GGC	Mercedes-Benz 811D	Robin Hood		C29F	1989	
089	F89GGC	Mercedes-Benz 811D	Robin Hood		C29F	1989	
090	F90GGC	Mercedes-Benz 811D	Robin Hood		C29F	1989	
091	RIB8432	Iveco Daily 49.10	Robin Hood		C12F	1989	
092	WPX448	Toyota Coaster HB31R	Caetano Optimo		C18F	1990	
093	165BXP	Mercedes-Benz 811D	Optare StarRider		C29F	1992	Ex Castleways, Winchcombe, 1991
094	672DYA	Toyota Coaster HDB30R	Caetano Optimo II		C21F	1991	Ex Welsh, Pontefract, 1992
303	D85DOT	Mercedes-Benz 609D	Robin Hood		C14F	1987	Ex Victoria Shuttle, SW1, 1991
330	SVO89	Volvo B10M-60	Plaxton Paramount 3500 III		C49FT	1990	Ex Park's, Hamilton, 1992
333	43FJF	Volvo B10M-60	Plaxton Paramount 3500 III		C49FT	1990	Ex Park's, Hamilton, 1992
334	RIB5084	Volvo B10M-60	Plaxton Paramount 3500 III		C49FT	1990	Ex Park's, Hamilton, 1992
336	RIB5086	Volvo B10M-60	Plaxton Paramount 3500 III		C49FT	1990	Ex Park's, Hamilton, 1992
337	G77RGG	Volvo B10M-60	Plaxton Paramount 3500 III		C49FT	1990	Ex Park's, Hamilton, 1992
338	G78RGG	Volvo B10M-60	Plaxton Paramount 3500 III		C49FT	1990	Ex Park's, Hamilton, 1992

341	OO1942	Volvo B10M-60		Plaxton Paramount 3500 III	C49FT	1991	Ex Wallace Arnold, Leeds, 1994	
342	RIB4315	LAG Panoramic		LAG	C32FT	1989	Ex AML, Hounslow, 1994	
901	RIB6195	Kassbohrer Setra S215HR		Kassbohrer Rational	C49FT	1987	Ex Naylor, London SE13, 1992	

Previous Registrations

165BXP	J361BNM		RIB5086	G86RGG	RIB7002	BAC551Y	E782MLB	OO1942, E181DBB
672DYA	J310KFP		RIB6195	D396BPE	RIB8432	F91JGJ	E783MLB	33LUG, E779VGK
43FJF	G43RGG		RIB6197	F81GGC	SVO89	G44RGG	E784MLB	672DYA, B164KNH
OO1942	H608VWR		RIB6198	F82GGC	ULL897	E200UWT	E785MLB	165BXP, E165KNH
RIB4315	A17AML,F504YNV		WPX448	G92LGK	E780MLB	43FJF, E778VGK		
RIB5084	G74RGG		RIB6199	F83GGC	E781MLB	SVO89, E180DBB		

Livery
Grey with red and blue relief.
H608UWR carries a revised livery style.

RALPH'S COACHES LTD

Ralph's Coaches Ltd, Middle Green Trading Estate, Middle Green, Langley, Slough, Berks, SL3 6BX

C851EML	Volvo B10M-46	Plaxton Bustler II	DP33F	1986	
C852EML	Volvo B10M-46	Plaxton Bustler II	DP33F	1986	
C853EML	Volvo B10M-46	Plaxton Bustler II	DP33F	1986	
C854EML	Volvo B10M-46	Plaxton Bustler II	DP33F	1986	
WSV478	Volvo B10M-46	Plaxton Paramount 3200 III	C39F	1987	
D251HFX	Volvo B10M-61	Plaxton Paramount 3500 III	C49FT	1987	Ex Armchair, Brentford, 1989
E742JAY	Toyota Coaster HB31R	Caetano Optimo	C18F	1988	Ex Sear, Staplehill, 1991
E580UHS	Volvo B10M-61	Plaxton Paramount 3500 III	C53F	1988	Ex Park's, Hamilton, 1989
F817TMD	Volvo B10M-60	Plaxton Paramount 3500 III	C56F	1989	
F818TMD	Volvo B10M-60	Plaxton Paramount 3500 III	C55F	1989	
F819TMD	Volvo B10M-60	Plaxton Paramount 3500 III	C53F	1989	
WSV468	Volvo B10M-60	Plaxton Paramount 3500 III	C56F	1990	
H394CFT	Toyota Coaster HDB30R	Caetano Optimo II	C21F	1991	
H16SHH	Mercedes-Benz 811D	G C Smith	C31F	1991	
H17SHH	Mercedes-Benz 811D	G C Smith	C31F	1991	
H18SHH	Mercedes-Benz 811D	G C Smith	C31F	1991	
H101VUB	DAF SB220LC550	Optare Delta	DP29D	1991	
H102VUB	DAF SB220LC550	Optare Delta	DP29D	1991	
H103VUB	DAF SB220LC550	Optare Delta	DP29D	1991	
H104VUB	DAF SB220LC550	Optare Delta	DP29D	1991	
H105VUB	DAF SB220LC550	Optare Delta	DP29D	1991	
H106VUB	DAF SB220LC550	Optare Delta	DP29D	1991	
K815EET	Volvo B10M-60	Van Hool Alizee HE	C48FT	1992	
K816EET	Volvo B10M-46	Van Hool Alizee HE	C36FT	1992	
K935GWR	Mercedes-Benz 814D	Optare StarRider	C27F	1992	
K936GWR	Mercedes-Benz 814D	Optare StarRider	C27F	1992	
K937GWR	Mercedes-Benz 814D	Optare StarRider	C27F	1992	
K938GWR	Mercedes-Benz 814D	Optare StarRider	C27F	1992	
K939GWR	Mercedes-Benz 814D	Optare StarRider	C27F	1992	
L62YJF	Volvo B6	Caetano Algarve II	C35F	1993	
L63YJF	Volvo B6	Caetano Algarve II	C35F	1993	
L990CRY	Toyota Coaster HZB50R	Caetano Optimo III	C18F	1994	
L991CRY	Toyota Coaster HZB50R	Caetano Optimo III	C18F	1994	
L992CRY	Toyota Coaster HZB50R	Caetano Optimo III	C18F	1994	
L672PWT	DAF SB220LC550	Optare Delta	DP29D	1994	
M231UKU	Volvo B10M-62	Plaxton Premiere 350 II	C48FT	1994	

Previous Registrations

WSV468	H161DJU	WSV478	From New

Livery
White and two tone blue.

Special Liveries
British Airports Authority (White, green and grey): H101-106VUB, L672PWT.
Holiday Inn Heathrow (Maroon and grey): L62YJF, L63YJF.
Marriott Hotel, Slough (Magenta): K935-939GWR.
Sheraton Heathrow Hotel (Metallic blue and silver): H16-18SHH.

About to pass New Scotland Yard in Victoria Street is Provence Private Hire C759CWX. Now that most National Express contractors have chosen Expressliners as their front line vehicles, many of these MCW Metroliners are appearing with independent operators. This single doored example was previously with Amberline of Speke. Scott Tillbrook

Following a recent staff competition to design a new company livery, R&I's 341 has appeared in this unique yet very pleasing livery based on the existing colour scheme. Acquired from Wallace Arnold in 1994, it had just entered Heathrow Airport on a private hire in September 1994 shortly before receiving a cherished registration. Colin Lloyd

Although R&I have small Kassbohrer Optimals in their fleet, 901 is the only full size Kassbohrer Setra operated with the Rational body. July 1993 finds the coach departing Victoria for Portsmouth on National Express route 075. Colin Lloyd

An April shower in Victoria Street welcomes Ralph's short length Volvo B10M-46 with bodywork by Van Hool. K816EET was delivered new in 1992 and carries the very effective revised livery afforded to the newer coaches. Colin Lloyd

With a rather angular style of G.C.Smith 31-seat body, Ralph's Coaches of Langley operate this Mercedes-Benz 811D on contract to the Sheraton Heathrow Hotel. H17SHH passes Heathrow police station on the East Ramp on its way into the airport in October 1994. Geoff Rixon

REDWING COACHES

Pullmanor Ltd, 145-147 Coldharbour Lane, London, SE5 9PD

E991KJF	Mercedes-Benz 0303-15R	Mercedes-Benz	C53F	1988	
E992KJF	Mercedes-Benz 0303-15R	Mercedes-Benz	C53F	1988	
E993KJF	Mercedes-Benz 0303-15R	Mercedes-Benz	C53F	1988	
E994KJF	Mercedes-Benz 0303-15R	Mercedes-Benz	C53F	1988	
E995KJF	Mercedes-Benz 0303-15R	Mercedes-Benz	C53F	1988	
F700PAY	Mercedes-Benz 0303-15R	Mercedes-Benz	C53F	1988	
F701PAY	Mercedes-Benz 0303-15R	Mercedes-Benz	C53F	1988	
F702PAY	Mercedes-Benz 0303-15R	Mercedes-Benz	C53F	1988	
F703PAY	Mercedes-Benz 0303-15R	Mercedes-Benz	C53F	1988	
F704PAY	Mercedes-Benz 0303-15R	Mercedes-Benz	C53F	1989	
F705PAY	Mercedes-Benz 0303-15R	Mercedes-Benz	C53F	1989	
F706PAY	Mercedes-Benz 0303-15R	Mercedes-Benz	C53F	1989	
F707PAY	Mercedes-Benz 0303-15R	Mercedes-Benz	C53F	1989	
F708PAY	Mercedes-Benz 0303-15R	Mercedes-Benz	C53F	1989	
F709PAY	Mercedes-Benz 0303-15R	Mercedes-Benz	C53F	1989	
J211DYL	Mercedes-Benz OH1628L	Jonckheere Deauville P599	C53F	1992	
J212DYL	Mercedes-Benz OH1628L	Jonckheere Deauville P599	C53F	1992	
J213DYL	Mercedes-Benz OH1628L	Jonckheere Deauville P599	C53F	1992	
J214DYL	Mercedes-Benz OH1628L	Jonckheere Deauville P599	C55F	1992	
J215DYL	Mercedes-Benz OH1628L	Jonckheere Deauville P599	C55F	1992	
J216DYL	Mercedes-Benz OH1628L	Jonckheere Deauville P599	C55F	1992	
K262FUV	Dennis Javelin 12SDA2117	Plaxton Premiere 320	C53F	1993	
K263FUV	Dennis Javelin 12SDA2117	Plaxton Premiere 320	C53F	1993	
K264FUV	Dennis Javelin 12SDA2117	Plaxton Premiere 320	C53F	1993	
K265FUV	Dennis Javelin 12SDA2115	Plaxton Premiere 320	C57F	1993	
K401STL	Kassbohrer Setra S210H	Kassbohrer Optimal	C35F	1993	Ex Spirit of London, Hounslow,1994
L270HJD	Volvo B10M-62	Plaxton Premiere 350 II	C50FT	1994	
L271HJD	Volvo B10M-62	Plaxton Premiere 350 II	C42FT	1994	
L272HJD	Volvo B10M-62	Plaxton Premiere 350 II	C50FT	1994	
L273HJD	Volvo B10M-62	Plaxton Premiere 350 II	C50FT	1994	
L274HJD	Volvo B10M-62	Plaxton Premiere 350 II	C50FT	1994	
L275HJD	Volvo B10M-62	Plaxton Premiere 350 II	C50FT	1994	
L276HJD	Volvo B10M-62	Plaxton Premiere 350 II	C50FT	1994	
M230LYT	Volvo B10M-62	Plaxton Premiere 350 II	C49F	1995	
M231LYT	Volvo B10M-62	Plaxton Premiere 350 II	C49FT	1995	
M232LYT	Volvo B10M-62	Plaxton Premiere 350 II	C49FT	1995	
M233LYT	Volvo B10M-62	Plaxton Premiere 350 II	C49FT	1995	
M234LYT	Volvo B10M-62	Plaxton Premiere 350 II	C49FT	1995	
M235LYT	Volvo B10M-62	Plaxton Premiere 350 II	C49FT	1995	

Livery
Red and cream.

Special Liveries
Evan Evans Tours (Red and cream) E992KJF, E994KJF, E995KJF & J211-6DYL.
Frames Rickards (Maroon with gold signwriting) E993 KJF.
Travel & Tourism International (White with red and black signwriting) F708PAY.

RELIANCE OF GRAVESEND

Reliance Coaches of Gravesend, 45 Darnley Road, Gravesend, Kent, DA11 0SD

PJI5634	Leyland Tiger TRCTL11/3R	Duple Dominant IV	C53F	1981	Ex Lincoln City Transport, 1988
DSU106	Leyland Tiger TRCTL11/3R	Plaxton Paramount 3200	C53F	1984	Ex Hills, Tredegar, 1989
PJI3531	Leyland Royal Tiger RTC	Leyland Doyen	C49F	1987	
PJI3533	Leyland Royal Tiger RTC	Leyland Doyen	C49F	1987	
PJI3532	Volvo B10M-61	Plaxton Paramount 3200 III	C53F	1988	
PJI8635	Volvo B10M-61	Plaxton Paramount 3500 III	C49F	1989	Ex Ambassador Travel, 1993
TIB7836	Volvo B10M-50	Van Hool Alizee SH	C49F	1990	Ex Harry Shaw, Coventry, 1993
H263GRY	Leyland Tiger TRBL10/3ARZA	Plaxton Paramount 3200 III	C53F	1991	
H264GRY	Leyland Tiger TRCL10/3RZM	Plaxton Paramount 3200 III	C53F	1991	
H265GRY	Leyland Tiger TR2R62C21Z6/8	Plaxton Paramount 3200 III	C53F	1991	
H266GRY	Leyland Tiger TR2R62C21Z6/8	Plaxton Paramount 3200 III	C53F	1991	

Previous Registrations

DSU106	A776WHB	PJI3533	D164HML	PJI8635	F103CCL
PJI3531	D162HML	PJI5634	JCW726W	TIB7836	G800CRW, 1KOV, G943EHP
PJI3532	E291OMG				

Livery
Various designs based on yellow or white.

PETER REYNOLDS COACHES

P.J.Reynolds, 35 Westbury Road, Northwood, Middx, HA6 3DB

CFS829S	Seddon Pennine VII	Alexander AY	B53F	1978	Ex Reynolds Diplomat, Bushey, 1990
EFS228S	Leyland Leopard PSU3E/4R	Alexander AT	C49F	1978	Ex Lothian, 1991
EFS229S	Leyland Leopard PSU3E/4R	Alexander AT	C49F	1978	Ex Lothian, 1991
EFS230S	Leyland Leopard PSU3E/4R	Alexander AT	C49F	1978	Ex Lothian, 1991
AHN391T	Leyland Leopard PSU3E/4R	Plaxton Supreme IV Express	C55F	1978	Ex Cleveland Transit, 1990
WJM808T	Leyland Leopard PSU3E/4R	Plaxton Supreme III Express	C46F	1979	Ex Monk & Allday, Lostwithiel, 1994
GGM66W	Leyland Leopard PSU3F/4R	Plaxton Supreme IV Express	C49F	1981	Ex Berks Bucks, 1991
ANA91Y	Leyland Leopard PSU5E/4R	Eastern Coach Works B51	DP57F	1982	Ex Williamson, Shrewsbury, 1992

Livery
Various.

REYNOLDS DIPLOMAT

R.Reynolds, 22 Bushey Hall Road, Bushey, Herts, WD2 2ED

✘ 278EPX	Volvo B58-61	Jonckheere Bermuda	C49FT	1981	Ex Webb, Highwood, 1991
RXI4598	DAF MB200DKTL600	Jonckheere Bermuda	C57F	1982	Ex Peter Reynolds, Northwood, 1990
ALJ557A	Mercedes-Benz 0303/15RHP	Mercedes-Benz	C47FT	1983	Ex Peter Reynolds, Northwood, 1990
KIJ56	Leyland Tiger TRCTL11/3R	Plaxton Paramount 3500	C50FT	1983	Ex Vanguard, Bedworth, 1993
RXI9280	DAF SB2300DHS585	Berkhof Esprite 350	C49FT	1983	Ex Lush & Hubbocks, Luton, 1990
B839NKA	Leyland Tiger TRCTL11/3RH	Plaxton Paramount 3500 II	C49FT	1985	Ex Blue Triangle, Bootle, 1993
C460CNG	Leyland Tiger TRCTL11/3RZ	Plaxton Paramount 3500 II	C49FT	1986	Ex Rosemary, Terrington St.Clements, 1993
D654SRM	Volvo B10M-61	Plaxton Paramount 3500 II	C55F	1986	Ex Messenger, Aspatria, 1994
J91JFR	Dennis Javelin 12SDA1929	Plaxton Paramount 3200 III LS	C57F	1991	Ex Grimshaw, Burnley, 1994
L2RDC	Mercedes-Benz 811D	Autobus Classique	C24F	1994	
L3RDC	Mercedes-Benz 814D	Autobus Classique	C33F	1994	

Previous Registrations

278EPX	WNV818W	KIJ56	WWA301Y	RXI9280	A648NOO
ALJ557A	PUL87Y	RXI4598	WRK12X	B839NKA	B27OBF, 4327PL, B457SFA, 449CLT

Livery
Green and white with gold relief.
J91JFR is white, silver and grey with black and red relief.

SSS

Spanish Speaking Services Ltd, 138 Eversholt Street, London, NW10 1BL

YAE473	Kassbohrer Setra S215HD	Kassbohrer Tornado	C49FT	1983	Ex Bebb, Llantwit Fardre, 1986
D701NUH	Kassbohrer Setra S215HR	Kassbohrer Rational	C53F	1987	Ex Bebb, Llantwit Fardre, 1986
E491GPK	Kassbohrer Setra S215HD	Kassbohrer Rational	C49FT	1988	Ex Fortmere, Uxbridge, 1991
F179OVL	Kassbohrer Setra S215HR	Kassbohrer Rational	C53F	1989	
G708LKW	Scania K93CRB	Plaxton Paramount 3500 III	C57F	1990	
✘ H878GTM	Mercedes-Benz 0303/15	Plaxton Paramount 3500 III	C55F	1991	
J62NTM	Mercedes-Benz 0303/15	Plaxton Paramount 3500 III	C55F	1992	
K436AVS	Plaxton 425	Lorraine	C55F	1993	
L372LHE	Scania K113CRB	Van Hool Alizee HE	C53F	1994	
L373LHE	Scania K113CRB	Van Hool Alizee HE	C53F	1994	

Previous Registration
YAE473   RAX23Y

Livery
White with red relief.
K436AVS carries ISS fleetnames.

Another operator accustomed to using smart and invariably clean vehicles is Redwing. An immaculate F705PAY is a Mercedes-Benz 0303 integral, one of fifteen such examples in the thirty nine strong operation. Colin Lloyd

Wearing the familiar livery of Evan Evans Tours is Redwing's J214DYL, one of the six rare Jonckheere Deauville P599 bodied Mercedes-Benz coaches bought new in 1992. May 1994 finds the vehicle outside Hampton Court Station awaiting passengers for the trip back to London. Geoff Rixon

One of a pair, this integral Leyland Royal Tiger Doyen is for many enthusiasts the epitome of a totally British built coach. PJI3531 had just completed its morning run into London and was returning to Kent via Vauxhall Bridge Road in August 1994. Reliance sold its commuter services to Kentish Bus in January 1995. Colin Lloyd

Finchley Road at Swiss Cottage and Reynolds Diplomat 278EPX climbs the gradient on its way home in May 1994. One of a pair of Jonckheere Bermudas operated, this vehicle is mounted on the Volvo B58 and was new in 1981, the year before this bodywork was replaced by the Jubilee range. **Keith Grimes**

In an effort to increase sales of the 0303 chassis in the UK, Mercedes-Benz gave body builders the option to build their own bodies on the Mercedes-Benz chassis. One of the results is this rare Plaxton Paramount 3500 bodied Mercedes-Benz 0303 owned by Spanish Speaking Services. Colin Lloyd

SCANCOACHES OF LONDON

Scancoaches Ltd, Unit 2 Radford Estate, Old Oak Lane, Harlesden, London, NW10 6UA

TIB8559	Scania K112CRS	Jonckheere Jubilee P50	C53F	1983	
TIB8560	Scania K112CRS	Jonckheere Jubilee P50	C53F	1984	
TIB8567	Scania K112CLS	Jonckheere Jubilee P599	C57F	1985	
TIB8568	Scania K112CRS	Jonckheere Jubilee P599	C51FT	1986	
TIB8571	Volvo B10M-61	Jonckheere Jubilee P599	C51F	1987	
TIB8572	Volvo B10M-61	Jonckheere Jubilee P599	C51FT	1987	
TIB8570	Scania K112CRS	Jonckheere Jubilee P50	C57F	1987	
E509KNV	Scania K112CRB	Jonckheere Jubilee P599	C39FT	1988	
E510KNV	Scania K112CRB	Jonckheere Jubilee P599	C41FT	1988	
E511KNV	Scania K112CRB	Jonckheere Jubilee P599	C57F	1988	
E512KNV	Scania K112CRB	Jonckheere Jubilee P599	C51FT	1988	
E513KNV	Scania K112CRB	Jonckheere Jubilee P599	C51FT	1988	
F867TNH	Volvo B10M-61	Caetano Algarve	C53F	1988	
F868TNH	Volvo B10M-61	Caetano Algarve	C53F	1988	
F869TNH	Volvo B10M-61	Caetano Algarve	C53F	1988	
TIB8573	Scania K113CRB	Jonckheere Deauville P599	C30FT	1989	
TIB8574	Scania K113CRB	Jonckheere Deauville P599	C30FT	1989	
F945RNV	Scania K113CRB	Jonckheere Deauville P599	C57F	1989	
F946RNV	Scania K113CRB	Jonckheere Deauville P599	C57F	1989	
F947RNV	Scania K113CRB	Jonckheere Deauville P599	C57F	1989	
F948RNV	Scania K113CRB	Jonckheere Deauville P599	C57F	1989	
F949RNV	Scania K113CRB	Jonckheere Deauville P599	C57F	1989	
G976LRP	Volvo B10M-60	Jonckheere Deauville P599	C53F	1990	
G977LRP	Volvo B10M-60	Jonckheere Deauville P599	C53F	1990	
G978LRP	Volvo B10M-60	Jonckheere Deauville P599	C53F	1990	
TIB8575	Volvo B10M-60	Jonckheere Deauville P599	C32FT	1990	
TIB8576	Volvo B10M-60	Jonckheere Deauville P599	C32FT	1990	
G164XJF	Toyota Coaster HB31R	Caetano Optimo	C18F	1990	
G165XJF	Toyota Coaster HB31R	Caetano Optimo	C18F	1990	
H61XBD	Volvo B10M-60	Jonckheere Deauville P599	C51FT	1991	
H62XBD	Volvo B10M-60	Jonckheere Deauville P599	C51FT	1991	
J78VTX	Kassbohrer Setra S215HD	Kassbohrer Tornado	C49FT	1992	Ex Travellers, Hounslow, 1994
L727MWW	Mercedes-Benz 814D	Optare StarRider	C29F	1993	
L528XUT	Volvo B10M-60	Jonckheere Deauville P599	C51FT	1993	
L529XUT	Volvo B10M-60	Jonckheere Deauville P599	C51FT	1993	
L530XUT	Volvo B10M-60	Jonckheere Deauville P599	C51FT	1993	
CAZ2043	Kassbohrer Setra S210H	Kassbohrer Optimal	C35F	1994	
CAZ2044	Kassbohrer Setra S210H	Kassbohrer Optimal	C35F	1994	
CAZ2045	Kassbohrer Setra S210H	Kassbohrer Optimal	C35F	1994	
CAZ2046	Kassbohrer Setra S210H	Kassbohrer Optimal	C35F	1994	
CAZ2047	Kassbohrer Setra S210H	Kassbohrer Optimal	C35F	1994	
L667PWT	Mercedes-Benz 814D	Optare StarRider	C29F	1994	
L668PWT	Mercedes-Benz 814D	Optare StarRider	C29F	1994	
L669PWT	Mercedes-Benz 814D	Optare StarRider	C29F	1994	

Previous Registrations

CAZ2043	From New	TIB8560	A116XNH	TIB8572	D98BNV
CAZ2044	From New	TIB8567	C409LRP	TIB8573	F943RNV
CAZ2045	From New	TIB8568	D323VVV	TIB8574	F944RNV
CAZ2046	From New	TIB8570	D325VVV	TIB8575	G979LRP
CAZ2047	From New	TIB8571	D97BNV	TIB8576	G980LRP
TIB8559	A127XNH				

Livery
White with blue relief.

SHIRE COACHES

M.W.Maney & W.J.Bowdrey, 31 Frogmoor, Park Street, St Albans, Herts, AL2 2NH

XRR615M	Leyland Leopard PSU3B/4R	Plaxton Panorama Elite III Exp	C53F	1973	Ex Universitybus, Aldenham, 1994
UXI8636	AEC Reliance 6U3ZR	Plaxton Panorama Elite III	C57F	1974	Ex Mini Trippers, Potters Bar, 1991
EAM463V	Bedford YMT	Caetano Alpha	C53F	1980	Ex Swann, Leicester, 1994
CDZ1699	Scania K112CRS	Plaxton Paramount 3500	C49FT	1984	Ex Snells, Newton Abbott, 1994
D358CBC	Mercedes-Benz 0303	Mercedes-Benz	C49FT	1987	Ex Roffey, Flimwell, 1994
D102ERU	DAF MB230DKFL615	Plaxton Paramount 3200 II	C53F	1986	Ex Price, Halesowen, 1992
D207VEV	Volvo B10M-61	Berkhof Esprite 350	C49FT	1987	Ex Appleby, Humberside, 1993
G478SYS	Hestair Duple 425 SDA1512	Duple 425	C53FT	1990	Ex Chapman, Airdrie, 1994
L577ULY	Ford Transit Executive	Ford	M7	1994	

Previous Registrations

CDZ1699	A112RMJ	EAM463V	DMR673V, ACH32A		UXI8636	UNK485N

Livery
White

SILVERGRAY

P.A. Ward, J.C. Silverwood & V.J. Keith, Bedfont Trading Estate, Bedfont Road, Bedfont, Middx. TW14 8EE

CAZ2050	Volvo B10M-61	Van Hool Astral	CH47/11FT	1984	Ex Showline, Abercynon, 1993
FIL9372	DAF SBR2300DHS570	Jonckheere Jubilee P90	CH9/7DT	1985	Ex Falcon, London NW5, 1994
MIW2408	Volvo B10M-61	Caetano Algarve	C11FT	1986	Ex Park's, Hamilton, 1991

Previous Registrations

CAZ2050	A549XUH	FIL9372	B499GBD	MIW2408	C102HUS

Livery
Silver with black signwriting

SKINNERS

F.N. & J.W. Skinner and B.J. Harvey, 15, Barrow Green Road, Oxted, Surrey, RH8 0NJ

661SKN	Bedford YMT	Plaxton Supreme IV	C53F	1979	
798SKN	Bedford YMT	Plaxton Supreme IV	C53F	1979	
6SKN	Kassbohrer Setra S215HD	Kassbohrer Tornado	C49FT	1983	
SKN418	Kassbohrer Setra S215H	Kassbohrer Optimal	C53F	1984	
B883AGJ	Mercedes-Benz L307D	Devon Conversions	M12	1985	
182SKN	Mercedes-Benz L608D	Robin Hood	C19	1985	
435SKN	Kassbohrer Setra S210HD	Kassbohrer Optimal	C35FT	1986	
747SKN	Mercedes-Benz 307D	Reeve Burgess	M12	1987	
G940EEH	MCW Metrorider MF154/14	MCW	C28F	1988	Ex Sherratt, Swynnerton, 1990
H330KCF	Dennis Javelin 11SDL1921	Duple 320	C55F	1991	Ex private owner, 1992
J872RPJ	MCW Metrorider MF156	MCW	C25F	1992	

Previous Registrations

6SKN	YPG974Y	661SKN	CMJ443T	798SKN	HRO447V
182SKN	B489CGN	747SKN	D676CFP	SKN418	A725HPF
435SKN	C855UPM				

Livery
Fawn with brown or pale green relief.

Scancoaches of London's intake of coaches in 1994 consisted of three new Optare StarRiders and five of these Kassbohrer Setra Optimals with short 35 seat bodies. All five, unusually for Scancoaches, were given select registrations from new as worn by CAZ2043 at Marble Arch in October 1994. Geoff Rixon

The characteristic low driving position of the Jonckheere Jubilee P599 is here shown to good effect, although the similar P50 has the same height body but with a high driving position. With Scania K112CRB chassis, Scancoaches E513KNV was crossing Oxford Circus in this June 1994 view. Colin Lloyd

One of only two non-European vehicles in the Scancoaches fleet is this Toyota Coaster, although the body is of course European built. About to enter Parliament Square, G165XJF was caught in Bridge Street, Westminster in May 1994. Colin Lloyd

Shire Coaches have built up a mixed assortment of vehicles since 1991 and now own eight coaches all with different chassis and five types of bodywork. D207VEV is a Berkhof Esprite 350 bodied Volvo B10M, the sister to the coach illustrated with Marshalls. It is seen turning into Elizabeth Bridge, Victoria in August 1994.
Colin Lloyd

Silvergray have a very interesting trio of coaches, the oldest of which is CAZ2050. Pictured at the company depot in Bedfont, this Volvo B10M is fitted with the rare Van Hool Astral body featuring the unusual rear lower deck saloon. Foreign travel accounts for a lot of the company's workload.
Geoff Rixon

Skinners are a family run business with a base in Oxted, Surrey specialising in private hires. Passing Westminster Abbey in St Margaret Street is Kassbohrer Setra S215H Optimal SKN418 on such a private hire in June 1994. Colin Lloyd

SMITH'S

W.H.V. & Mrs V. Smith, 59, Staplehurst Road, Sittingbourne, Kent, ME10 2NY

Coach fleet

AKL640T	Ford R1114	Duple Dominant II Express	C53F	1978	
JFD288V	Ford R1114	Duple Dominant II	C53F	1979	Ex Olsen, Strood, 1980
OHA467W	Ford R1114	Plaxton Supreme IV	C53F	1980	Ex Parry, Cheslyn Hay, 1982
A638LKO	Ward Dalesman TV8-640	Plaxton Paramount 3200	C57F	1983	
LIB7133	Leyland Tiger TRCTL11/3R	Plaxton Paramount 3500	C53F	1984	Ex Hills, Tredegar, 1988
LIB7134	Leyland Tiger TRCTL11/3R	Plaxton Paramount 3500	C53F	1984	Ex Hills, Tredegar, 1988
B164TKL	Leyland Tiger TRCTL11/3R	Plaxton Paramount 3200	C57F	1984	
B46XKJ	Leyland Tiger TRCTL11/3R	Plaxton Paramount 3500	C53F	1985	
MIB526	Leyland Royal Tiger RTC	Leyland Doyen	C48FT	1986	Ex Fishwick, Leyland, 1988
D330NTG	Leyland Tiger TRCTL11/3RZ	Jonckheere Jubilee P599	C51FT	1986	Ex Thomas, Clydach Vale, 1992
E75VKO	Leyland Tiger TRCTL11/3RZ	Plaxton Paramount 3200 III	C57F	1987	
E76VKO	Leyland Tiger TRCTL11/3RZ	Plaxton Paramount 3200 III	C57F	1987	
F337JTN	Toyota Coaster HB31R	Caetano Optimo	C21F	1088	Ex Proctor, Bedale, 1993
F22YBO	Kassbohrer Setra S215HDI	Kassbohrer Tornado	C49FT	1989	Ex Bebb, Llantwit Fardre, 1991
G957WNR	Dennis Javelin 12SDA1907	Plaxton Paramount 3200 III	C57F	1990	Ex Reliance, Gravesend, 1993
G958WNR	Dennis Javelin 12SDA1907	Plaxton Paramount 3200 III	C57F	1990	Ex Reliance, Gravesend, 1993

Previous Registrations
LIB7133	A782WHB	MIB526	C752MFR
LIB7134	A586WNY	D330NTG	C335HHB

Livery
Black, white and grey.

Smith's of Sittingbourne run daily commuter services into the heart of London with a fleet consisting mainly of British coaches. One of the odd ones is Kassbohrer Setra F22YBO in Victoria Street trying to get out of crawler gear en route to Kent. Colin Lloyd

SPEEDLINK

Speedlink Airport Services Ltd, 106-107 Ashfield House, Gatwick Airport, West Sussex, RH6 0JH

BTL11	B111KPF	Leyland Tiger TRCTL11/3R	Berkhof Everest 370	C53F	1984	Ex London Country S.W. 1989
BTL15	B115KPF	Leyland Tiger TRCTL11/3R	Berkhof Everest 370	C53F	1984	Ex London Country S.W. 1989
BTL17	B117KPF	Leyland Tiger TRCTL11/3R	Berkhof Everest 370	C53F	1984	Ex London Country S.W. 1989
BTL19	B119KPF	Leyland Tiger TRCTL11/3R	Berkhof Everest 370	C53F	1984	Ex London Country S.W. 1989
BTL20	B120KPF	Leyland Tiger TRCTL11/3R	Berkhof Everest 370	C53F	1984	Ex London Country S.W. 1989
BTL30	C130PPE	Leyland Tiger TRCTL11/3R	Berkhof Everest 370	C49FT	1985	Ex London Country S.W. 1989

Fleet	Reg	Chassis	Body	Seats	Year	Notes
BTL33	C133PPE	Leyland Tiger TRCTL11/3R	Berkhof Everest 370	C49FT	1985	Ex London Country S.W. 1989
BTL35	C135SPB	Leyland Tiger TRCTL11/3R	Berkhof Everest 370	C49FT	1985	Ex London Country S.W. 1989
BTL46	HIL6246	Leyland Tiger TRCTL11/3R	Berkhof Everest 370	C49FT	1985	Ex London Country S.W. 1989
C1	J633KGB	Toyota Coaster HDB30R	Caetano Optimo II	C21F	1992	Ex Express Travel, Perth, 1993
S1	J111SAS	Scania K113CRB	Van Hool Alizee SH	C35FT	1992	
S2	J222SAS	Scania K113CRB	Van Hool Alizee SH	C35FT	1992	
S3	J333SAS	Scania K113CRB	Van Hool Alizee SH	C35FT	1992	
S4	J444SAS	Scania K113CRB	Van Hool Alizee SH	C35FT	1992	
S5	J555SAS	Scania K113CRB	Van Hool Alizee SH	C35FT	1992	
S6	K66SAS	Scania K113CRB	Van Hool Alizee SH	C35FT	1993	
S7	K77SAS	Scania K113CRB	Van Hool Alizee SH	C35FT	1993	
S8	K88SAS	Scania K113CRB	Van Hool Alizee SH	C35FT	1993	
S9	K99SAS	Scania K113CRB	Van Hool Alizee SH	C37FT	1993	
S10	K100SAS	Scania K113CRB	Van Hool Alizee SH	C35FT	1993	
S11	L10SAS	Scania K113CRB	Van Hool Alizee SH	C35FT	1993	
S12	L2SAS	Scania K113CRB	Van Hool Alizee SH	C35FT	1993	
S13	L3SAS	Scania K113CRB	Van Hool Alizee SH	C35FT	1993	
S14	L4SAS	Scania K113CRB	Van Hool Alizee SH	C35FT	1993	
S15	L5SAS	Scania K113CRB	Van Hool Alizee SH	C35FT	1993	
S44	L44SAS	Scania K113CRB	Plaxton Premiere 320	C47FT	1993	
S55	L55SAS	Scania K113CRB	Plaxton Premiere 320	C47FT	1993	
SP1	F431GWG	Scania K93CRB	Plaxton Paramount 3200 III LS	C49FT	1989	Ex A & R, Bedfont, 1993
SP2	G780CFA	Scania K93CRB	Plaxton Paramount 3200 III LS	C53FT	1990	Ex Happy Days, Woodseaves, 1993
SP3	G803RNC	Scania K93CRB	Plaxton Paramount 3200 III LS	C53F	1989	Ex Shearings, Wigan, 1993
SP4	G804RNC	Scania K93CRB	Plaxton Paramount 3200 III LS	C53F	1989	Ex Shearings, Wigan, 1993
T1	L848SFG	Toyota Lite-Ace	Toyota	M..	1993	
T4	F634UBL	Leyland Tiger TRCL10/3ARZA	Plaxton Paramount 3500 III	C53F	1989	Ex Berks Bucks, 1993
T5	F635UBL	Leyland Tiger TRCL10/3ARZA	Plaxton Paramount 3500 III	C53F	1989	Ex Berks Bucks, 1993
V1	G801BPG	Volvo B10M-60	Plaxton Paramount 3500 III	C37FT	1989	
V2	G802BPG	Volvo B10M-60	Plaxton Paramount 3500 III	C37FT	1989	
V3	G803BPG	Volvo B10M-60	Plaxton Paramount 3500 III	C37FT	1989	
V4	G804BPG	Volvo B10M-60	Plaxton Paramount 3500 III	C37FT	1989	
V5	G805BPG	Volvo B10M-60	Plaxton Paramount 3500 III	C37FT	1989	
V6	G806BPG	Volvo B10M-60	Plaxton Paramount 3500 III	C37FT	1989	
V7	G807BPG	Volvo B10M-60	Plaxton Paramount 3500 III	C37FT	1989	
V8	G808BPG	Volvo B10M-60	Plaxton Paramount 3500 III	C37FT	1989	
V9	G809BPG	Volvo B10M-60	Plaxton Paramount 3500 III	C37FT	1989	
V10	G810BPG	Volvo B10M-60	Plaxton Paramount 3500 III	C37FT	1989	
V11	G811BPG	Volvo B10M-60	Plaxton Paramount 3500 III	C37FT	1989	
V12	G812BPG	Volvo B10M-60	Plaxton Paramount 3500 III	C37FT	1989	
V13	G813BPG	Volvo B10M-60	Plaxton Paramount 3500 III	C37FT	1989	
V14	G814BPG	Volvo B10M-60	Plaxton Paramount 3500 III	C37FT	1989	
V15	G815BPG	Volvo B10M-60	Plaxton Paramount 3500 III	C37FT	1989	
V16	G816BPG	Volvo B10M-60	Plaxton Paramount 3500 III	C37FT	1989	
V17	G817BPG	Volvo B10M-60	Plaxton Paramount 3500 III	C37FT	1989	
V18	K80SAS	Volvo B10M-60	Plaxton Expressliner II	C49FT	1993	
V19	K90SAS	Volvo B10M-60	Plaxton Expressliner II	C46FT	1993	
V20	K200SAS	Volvo B10M-60	Plaxton Expressliner II	C46FT	1993	
V51	G251VPK	Volvo B10M-60	Plaxton Expressliner	C46FT	1990	
V52	G252VPK	Volvo B10M-60	Plaxton Expressliner	C46FT	1990	
V53	G253VPK	Volvo B10M-60	Plaxton Expressliner	C46FT	1990	
V54	G254VPK	Volvo B10M-60	Plaxton Expressliner	C46FT	1990	
V55	G255VPK	Volvo B10M-60	Plaxton Expressliner	C46FT	1990	

On order for 1995 are five Volvo B10M/Plaxton Premiere 350 coaches.

Previous Registration
HIL6246   C146SPB

Liveries
Air Link (Blue and silver with red, blue, orange and white relief): V8, 10, 11, 13.
British Airways Contracts (Blue and gold): C1.
Flightline (Green and grey with yellow, white and red relief): BTL11, 15, 17, 19, 20.
Jetlink (Green and grey with green, yellow and red relief): BTL30, 33, 35, 46, S44, S63, SP1, 2, 4, T5.
Heathrow-Gatwick Speedlink (Blue and white with red and yellow relief): S1-15, V2-4, 9.
Heathrow-Stansted Speedlink (Blue and white with red and yellow relief): V5-7.
National Express (White with red and blue stripes): S55 & V18.
National Express Rapide (White with red and blue stripes): V19, 20, 51-55.
Virgin Atlantic (Red with white relief): V1.
White: T4.
Woking-Heathrow Railair (Blue and grey with red, yellow and white relief): V12, 14-7.

Terminal 2 at Heathrow Airport, where Speedlink Airport Services solitary Toyota Coaster C1 (J633KGB) illustrates its Caetano Optimo II midi-coach body. Carrying the British Airways contracts livery of dark blue and gold, it is usually to be found at Gatwick. *Colin Lloyd*

The new standard vehicles for the Speedlink routes are Scania K113s with the high-floor version of the Van Hool Alizee body. They form the majority of the S class with S12 (L2SAS) seen here passing Heathrow coach station in November 1994. *Colin Lloyd*

Also within the S class of coaches are a pair of these Plaxton Premiere 320 bodied Scania K113s. S44 carries the latest Jetlink livery incorporating the red diagonal stripe at the rear end. Heathrow coach station is the location in September 1994. *Colin Lloyd*

The latest innovation in the ever expanding Speedlink Airport Services list of routes is the Airlink service linking Gatwick with East Midlands Airport via Heathrow. Adorned in the new dedicated livery is V8, a Volvo B10M with Plaxton Paramount body of 1989 vintage entering Heathrow coach station in September 1994. *Colin Lloyd*

Railair coaches ply Speedlink's trade between Heathrow and Woking. Operated in conjunction with Network South East, the service enables through journeys to be made from a host of towns as listed on the side of V12 at Heathrow bus station. *David Savage*

By far the majority of the Spirit of London vehicles now carry SOL select registrations, some re-registered and some from new. A14SOL was given its plate from new and is a MAN 10.180 with Caetano Algarve bodywork. November 1994 saw this midicoach passing the Houses of Parliament in St Margaret Street Westminster. Colin Lloyd

SPIRIT OF LONDON

Spirit of London Ltd, 27a Spring Grove Road, Hounslow, Middx, TW3 4BE

MDS241V	Leyland Leopard PSU5C/4R	Van Hool Aragon	C57F	1980	Ex Camm, Nottingham, 1994
E460ANC	Mercedes-Benz 507D	Made To Measure	C16F	1988	
A3SOL	LAG Panoramic	LAG	C49FT	1988	
A8SOL	LAG Panoramic	LAG	C49FT	1988	
A2SOL	LAG Panoramic	LAG	C49FT	1988	Ex Gaincrest, Bedfont, 1990
A10SOL	Toyota Coaster HB31R	Caetano Optimo	C18F	1990	
A14SOL	MAN 10.180	Caetano Algarve	C31FT	1992	
A15SOL	Toyota Coaster HDB30R	Caetano Optimo II	C18F	1992	
A16SOL	Fleur-de-Lys Lincoln 700/50	Fleur-de-Lys	C17F	1992	
A7SOL	Toyota Coaster HDB30R	Caetano Optimo II	C18F	1993	
K121OCT	Kassbohrer Setra S215HD	Kassbohrer Tornado	C35F	1993	

Previous Registrations

A2SOL	F22WNH	A8SOL	F618VNH	A14SOL	From New
A3SOL	E397MVV			A15SOL	From New
A7SOL	From New	A10SOL	G620YUT	A16SOL	From New

Livery
White. A16SOL is maroon and cream.

STARLINE

J.P. Mullany, Clarendon Garage, Cardiff Road, Watford, Herts, WD1 8DG

OJD143R	Leyland Fleetline FE30AGR	Park Royal	H45/27D	1976	Ex London Buses, 1990
GGD669T	Volvo B58-61	Plaxton Supreme IV	C57F	1979	Ex Safford, Little Gransden, 1985
HFX410V	Ford R1114	Plaxton Supreme IV	C49F	1980	Ex Hampton, Abbots Langley, 1987
KBC3V	Volvo B58-61	Plaxton Supreme IV	C57F	1980	Ex Ellis, Wembley Park, 1987
YDN504	Mercedes-Benz L307D	Reeve Burgess	M12	1983	Ex Simmonds, Letchworth, 1989
EBZ6294	Volvo B10M-61	Duple Laser	C57F	1983	Ex Link Line, London NW10, 1987
EBZ6295	Volvo B10M-61	Plaxton Paramount 3500	C57F	1983	Ex Skill, Nottingham, 1989
EBZ6296	Volvo B10M-61	Plaxton Paramount 3500	C57F	1983	Ex Skill, Sheffield, 1989
FDZ4730	Volvo B10M-61	Van Hool Alizee	C53F	1984	Ex Shearings, Wigan, 1990
FDZ5348	Volvo B10M-61	Van Hool Alizee	C53F	1984	Ex Shearings, Wigan, 1991
B21CYS	Mercedes-Benz L307D	Reeve Burgess	M12	1985	Ex Barrett, Great Mongeham, 1992

C938RPK	Mercedes-Benz L608D	Coachcraft	C21F	1986	
D317MNC	Mercedes-Benz 609D	Made To Measure	C27F	1987	Ex Flowers, Ashley Green, 1990
D910RBU	Scania K112CRS	Van Hool Alizee	C53FT	1987	Ex TRJ, Golborne, 1994
E41MMT	Mercedes-Benz 609D	Reeve Burgess	B19F	1987	
E890FOY	Talbot Express	Dormobile	B17FL	1988	Ex Welwyn Hatfield District Council, 1991
F727EKR	Freight-Rover Sherpa	Dormobile Routemaker	B21F	1989	Ex Blue Moon, Watford, 1993
F796FKU	Mercedes-Benz 811D	Whittaker	C24F	1989	
H254LOX	Mercedes-Benz 709D	....	C24FL	1991	Ex Blytheswood Motors, Glasgow, 1994

Named Vehicles
GGD669T Emerald Star
KBC3V   The North Star

Previous Registrations

EBZ6294	MSU598Y, EJV248, FLB453Y	EBZ6296	YNN30Y	FDZ5348	A180MNE
EBZ6295	YNN31Y	FDZ4730	A179MNE	YDN504	HBH420Y

Livery
White with blue and yellow relief

STORT VALLEY

Stort Valley Coaches Ltd, 160 Dunmow Road, Bishops Stortford, Herts, CM23 5HW

THM601M	Daimler Fleetline CRL6	MCW	H47/32F	1973	Ex Gemini, Bishops Stortford, 1993
SIB7358	Bedford YRQ	Plaxton Panorama Elite III	C45F	1975	Ex Gemini, Bishops Stortford, 1993
LRU822	Bedford YMT	Plaxton Supreme III Express	C53F	1977	Ex Jason, St Mary Cray, 1993
SDA525S	Leyland Fleetline FE30AGR	MCW	H47/33F	1977	Ex Wealden-Beeline, Five Oak Green, 1994
THX285S	Leyland Fleetline FE30ALRSp	MCW	H44/24D	1977	Ex Jason, St Mary Cray, 1993
CRW518T	Bedford YMT	Plaxton Supreme IV	C53F	1978	Ex Jason, St Mary Cray, 1993
SIB7359	Volvo B58-61	Plaxton Supreme IV	C53F	1980	Ex Rigby, Lathom, 1993
SIB7356	DAF MB200DKTL600	Plaxton Supreme IV	C51F	1982	Ex Gemini, Bishops Stortford, 1993
SIB7357	Van Hool T818	Van Hool Astron	CH50/10FT	1983	Ex Evag Cannon, Bolton, 1993
2447MT	Leyland Tiger TRCTL11/3R	Jonckheere Jubilee P50	C51FT	1984	Ex Mason, Hinckley, 1993
542HKD	Volvo B10M-61	Berkhof Espirit 350	C49FT	1984	Ex Hilton, Newton-le-Willows, 1994
C126PPE	Leyland Tiger TRCTL11/3RH	Berkhof Everest 370	C49FT	1985	Ex Speedlink, 1993
C131PPE	Leyland Tiger TRCTL11/3RH	Berkhof Everest 370	C49FT	1986	Ex Speedlink, 1994
C134SPB	Leyland Tiger TRCTL11/3RH	Berkhof Everest 370	C49FT	1986	Ex Speedlink, 1994

Previous Registrations

2447MT	A527BNT	SIB7356	TND428X		SIB7359	FAA358W, 386BUO
542HKD	A574RVW	SIB7357	TUH793Y, NIW6474, TUH793Y		CRW518T	CRW519T
LRU822	RGS88R	SIB7358	JVS935N			

Livery
White with green and grey relief.

SUNBURY COACHES

Sunbury Coaches Ltd, 74 Kenyngton Drive, Sunbury, Surrey, TW16 7RX

DJF632T	Bedford YMT	Plaxton Supreme IV	C53F	1979	Ex Jones, Laleham, 1988
EPC921V	Bedford YMT	Plaxton Dominant II	C53F	1979	Ex Jones, Laleham, 1988
BGS301X	Bedford YMT	Plaxton Supreme V	C53F	1982	Ex Harding, Betchworth, 1987
TVH137X	Ford R1014	Plaxton Supreme V	C35F	1982	Ex Chivers, Elstead, 1990
UPC63X	Mercedes-Benz L508DG	Robin Hood	C19F	1982	Ex Bicknell's, Godalming, 1987
NYS58Y	Leyland Tiger TRCTL11/3R	Van Hool Alizee H	C52F	1983	Ex Mitchell, Plean, 1991
B339AMH	Leyland Tiger TRCTL11/3R	Van Hool Alizee H	C53F	1985	Ex Worthing Coaches, 1991
B125KPF	Leyland Tiger TRCTL11/3RH	Berkhof Everest 370	C53F	1985	Ex Northumbria, 1993
HIL6754	Volvo B10M-61	Jonckheere Jubilee P599	C53F	1983	Ex Dodsworth, Boroughbridge, 1994

Previous Registration
HIL6754   A307XHE

Livery
White, turquoise and navy blue.

Spirit of London purchased this 17 seat Fluer-de-Lys in 1992 after its launch at the Bus and Coach Show. With select registration A16SOL from new, this vehicle remains unique in the London area and was captured in between jobs at the company depot in Spring Grove Road Hounslow on a sunny late September day in 1994. Geoff Rixon

Duple's Dominant family finally came to an end in 1982 when replaced by the Laser and Caribbean range. Representing the original Laser, which was produced for two years, is EBZ6294 of Mullany's Starline seen turning in Harrow Weald in March 1994. Colin Lloyd

During the past few years, the commuter service linking London with Bishops Stortford has seen a marked improvement in the rolling stock used. Entering Parliament Square in March 1994, SIB7357 is a scarce integral Van Hool T818 Astron used regularly by Stort Valley. Colin Lloyd

London Country was the largest British purchaser of the Berkhof Everest body, amassing fifty three on Leyland Tiger chassis. With the demise of many Green Line services, many have now ended up with small operators such as this example (former BTL25) with Sunbury Coaches. Having just been repainted, B125KPF is seen at the Shepperton depot in October 1994. Geoff Rixo

SWALLOW COACH COMPANY

Swallow Coach Company Ltd, 5 Orwell Close, Manor Way, Rainham, Essex, RM13 8UB

Reg	Chassis	Body	Type	Year	History
FFB358	Bedford SBG	Duple Vega	C38F	1955	Ex Purnell, West Rudham, 1988
FHW154D	Bristol MW6G	Eastern Coach Works	C39F	1966	Ex private owner, 1994
8056UA	Leyland Leopard PSU3B/4R	Willowbrook Crusader (1990)	C53F	1972	Ex Bygone, Biddendon, 1994
MFN44R	Bristol VRT/SL3/6LXB	Eastern Coach Works	H43/31F	1976	Ex Winson, Loughborough, 1994
JIL5284	Ford R1014	Duple Dominant II	C35F	1979	Ex Phillips, Crediton, 1992
JIL5283	Leyland Leopard PSU5C/4R	Duple Dominant II	C57F	1979	Ex O'Neill, Darwen, 1994
JIL5285	Leyland Leopard PSU3E/4R	Duple Dominant II Express	C53F	1979	Ex Hyndburn, 1994
JIL5286	Leyland Leopard PSU5C/4R	Duple Dominant II	C57F	1979	Ex Hyndburn, 1994
JIL5287	Ford R1114	Plaxton Supreme IV Express	C53F	1980	Ex Bolton, Farnham, 1990
JIL5288	Leyland Leopard PSU3E/4R	Plaxton Supreme V Express	C48F	1981	Ex United Counties, 1990
UAU227X	DAF MB200DKTL600	Plaxton Supreme V	C52F	1982	Ex Oakfield, Enfield, 1994
A100RGS	Bedford YNT	Wright Contour	C57F	1984	Ex Cedar, Bedford, 1993
B458WHJ	MCW Metroliner CR126/9	MCW	C51F	1984	Ex Alder Valley, 1991
B460WHJ	MCW Metroliner CR126/9	MCW	C51F	1984	Ex Alder Valley, 1991
B61DMB	Bova FHD12-280	Bova Futura	C49FT	1985	Ex Edmunds, Rassau, 1991
B872UST	Leyland Tiger TRCTL11/3RH	Duple Laser 2	C46Ft	1985	Ex White Rose, Castleford, 1993
C174KET	Auwaerter Neoplan N122/3	Auwaerter Skyliner	CH57/20CT	1986	Ex Yorkshire Voyager,1992
D578EWS	Freight Rover Sherpa 395	Dormobile	B16F	1986	Ex Really Nice, Berkhamsted, 1990
D871NVS	Freight Rover Sherpa 374	Dormobile	B16F	1986	Ex Powney, Aintree,1990
D801ALR	Bedford YMP	Plaxton Paramount 3200 III	C35F	1987	Ex Channel Coachways, London E2, 1993
E205EPB	Hestair Duple 425 SDA1510	Duple 425	C57F	1987	Ex Reading Transport, 1993
E565YBU	Mercedes-Benz 709D	Reeve Burgess Beaver	B25F	1988	Ex Star Line, Knutsford, 1993
F100CWG	Scania K92CRB	Van Hool Alizee	C55F	1988	Ex Shaw, Maxey, 1994
GIL3270	DAF SB3000DKV601	Caetano Algarve	C49FT	1989	Ex Wilson, Carnwath, 1994
F888SMU	Volvo B10M-61	Van Hool Alizee H	C53F	1989	
G650LWF	Volvo B10M-60	Ikarus Blue Danube 336	C53FT	1989	
H68BKM	Ford Transit	Crystals	C16F	1990	Ex Chambers, Upminster, 1994

Named Vehicle
A100RGS	Terrible Terry
C174KET	Gemma
E205EPB	Crafty Carl
F100CWG	Lucky Lee
F888SMU	Tricky Ricky

Previous Registrations
GIL3270	F207PNR	JIL5285	YHB20T	JIL5287	NVT452W	
JIL5283	BNB238T	JIL5286	DAK219V	JIL5288	MAP344W, XLD244, OUF56W	
JIL5284	AWA724T	8056UA	YDF323K			

Livery
White or white and blue.

TELLINGS GOLDEN MILLER / SHEENWAY

Tellings Golden Miller Ltd, 20a Wintersells Road, Byfleet, Surrey, KT14 7LF

Reg	Chassis	Body	Type	Year	History
ULA485W	Volvo B58-61	Plaxton Supreme IV	C55F	1981	Ex Gales, Haslemere, 1994
DKX111X	Volvo B10M-61	Plaxton Supreme IV	C57F	1982	Ex Link Line, Harlesden, 1994
A388XMC	Volvo B10M-61	Plaxton Paramount 3500	C53F	1984	Ex Sheenway, London W14, 1991
C97AUB	Ford Transit 190D	Carlyle	B20F	1986	Ex Stevensons, 1994
C89NNV	Volvo B10M-61	Caetano Stagecoach	B57F	1985	Ex Golden Miller, Byfleet, 1987
C456SJU	Ford Transit 190D	Robin Hood	B16F	1985	Ex Midland Fox, 1994
C467TAY	Ford Transit 190D	Dormobile	B16F	1985	Ex Midland Fox, 1993

C502TJF	Ford Transit 190D	Alexander	B16F	1985	Ex Midland Fox, 1990
C526TJF	Ford Transit 190D	Rootes	B16F	1986	Ex Midland Fox, 1991
C35WBF	Ford Transit 190D	Dormobile	B16F	1986	Ex Bluebird, Grangetown, 1994
C669XRU	Volvo B10M-61	Plaxton Paramount 3500 II	C49FT	1986	Ex Sheenway, London W14, 1991
D328VVV	Volvo B10M-61	Jonckheere Jubilee P599	C51FT	1987	
E224PWY	MCW Metrorider MF150/34	MCW	DP23F	1987	
E232PWY	MCW Metrorider MF150/41	MCW	B23F	1987	Ex Bluebird, Grangetown, 1994
E804UDT	MCW Metrorider MF150/15	MCW	B23F	1987	Ex Stevensons, 1994
E807UDT	MCW Metrorider MF150/15	MCW	B23F	1987	Ex Stevensons, 1994
E604VKC	MCW Metrorider MF150/40	MCW	B23F	1987	Ex Bluebird, Grangetown, 1994
F790GNA	Leyland Tiger TRCL10/3ARZ	Duple 320	C53F	1989	Ex Shearings, Wigan, 1994
F801TMD	Volvo B10M-60	Van Hool Alizee H	C48FT	1989	
✗ F807TMD	Volvo B10M-60	Van Hool Alizee H	C52F	1989	
F808TMD	Volvo B10M-60	Van Hool Alizee H	C52F	1989	
F810TMD	Volvo B10M-60	Van Hool Alizee H	C52F	1989	
F811TMD	Volvo B10M-60	Van Hool Alizee H	C52F	1989	
H274GRY	Toyota Coaster HDB30R	Caetano Optimo II	C18F	1991	
H275GRY	Toyota Coaster HDB30R	Caetano Optimo II	C18F	1991	
H659UWR	Volvo B10M-60	Plaxton Paramount 3500 III	C51F	1991	Ex Wallace Arnold, Leeds, 1994
J408AWF	Volvo B10M-60	Van Hool Alizee H	C34FT	1992	
J409AWF	Volvo B10M-60	Van Hool Alizee H	C48FT	1992	
J93UBL	Dennis Javelin 10SDA2119	Berkhof Excellence 1000	C28FT	1992	
L10TGM	Volvo B10M-62	Jonckheere Deauville 45L	C51FT	1994	
✗ L20TGM	Volvo B10M-62	Jonckheere Deauville 45L	C51FT	1994	

On order;- Two Volvo/Jonckheere, three Dennis Javelin/Plaxton Premiere (one C53F two C57F) and a Toyota/Optimo III minicoach.

Previous Registration
ULA485W UGG916W, CCC257 DKX111X VCX411X, 403NMM

Livery
White, blue and yellow.

Special Liveries
Sheenway (White with pink and mauve relief);- A388XMC, C669XRU, J93UBL.
Gullivers Travel Agency (White with blue signwriting);- F807TMD, F808TMD.

EDWARD THOMAS & SON

Ivan Edward Thomas, 442 Chessington Road, West Ewell, Surrey, KT19 9EJ

NRG168M	Leyland Atlantean AN68/1R	Alexander AL	H45/29D	1973	Acquired 1994
JWO179P	Bedford YRT	Plaxton Supreme	C53F	1976	Ex Wiffen, London, SW15, 1992
RHC51S	AEC Reliance 6U2R	Plaxton Supreme III	C51F	1977	Ex Stanbridge, Turners Hill, 1992
435UPD	AEC Reliance 6U3ZR	Plaxton Supreme III	C53F	1978	
XPF856S	Leyland Leopard PSU5C/4R	Plaxton Supreme III	C57F	1978	Ex Felicita, Gillingham, 1984
APM118T	AEC Reliance 6U2R	Plaxton Supreme IV Exp	C53F	1979	Ex Oxon Travel, Bicester, 1994
✗ 267PPH	Leyland Leopard PSU5C/4R	Plaxton Supreme IV	C57F	1979	Ex Frames Rickards, Brentford, 1986
YPL63T	AEC Reliance 6U2R	Duple Dominant II Express	C53F	1979	Ex Stanbridge, Turners Hill, 1994
160CLT	Leyland Tiger TRCTL11/3R	Plaxton Supreme V	C53F	1982	Ex London Country North West, 1989
HIL4017	Leyland Tiger TRCTL11/3R	Plaxton Supreme V	C53F	1982	
HIL3207	Leyland Tiger TRCTL11/3R	Plaxton Paramount 3200	C53F	1983	
A518LPP	Leyland Tiger TRCTL11/3R	Plaxton Paramount 3200	C53F	1983	Ex Frames Rickards, Brentford, 1989
H312HPF	Leyland Tiger TRCTL11/3R	Van Hool Alizee (1990)	C53F	1983	Ex MOD, 1990 (Chassis Only)
A51GPG	Leyland Tiger TRCTL11/3R	Plaxton Paramount 3200	C53F	1984	
C913UPB	Leyland Tiger TRCTL11/3R	Plaxton Paramount 3200	C53F	1986	

Previous Registrations
160CLT	SMY629X	267PPH	KBH842V	XPF856S	XKK184S, 8794R
HIL3207	APJ445Y	435UPD	WPJ455S	H312HPF	20KB76
HIL4017	UPE755X				

Livery
Two tone green and cream or green and cream.

109

Providing a refreshing change to many coach fleets is Swallow of Rainham. The variety of vehicles owned ranges enormously as these two examples show. Here is JIL5284, a 1979 Ford R1014 with handy 35-seat Duple Dominant II body shortened by Tricentrol to midicoach length. November 1994 finds it parked opposite the Department of Transport Headquarters in Marsham Street. *Colin Lloyd*

Representing one of the higher specification coaches in the Swallow fleet is this MCW Metroliner. One of only 42 single deck Metroliners built, 21 were of high floor design and called the Hiliner. The other half were 3.2 metres high and built with two different frontal designs. Acquired in 1991 from Alder Valley, B460WHJ stands in Old Kent Road. *David Savage*

Carrying the standard Tellings Golden Miller livery is this, the latest addition to the Byfleet based operation, a Jonckheere Deauville 45L bodied Volvo B10M-62 with side mounted radiator. Victoria Street Westminster sets the scene in September 1994. *Colin Lloyd*

Sheenway is a wholly owned subsidiary of Tellings Golden Miller and three of the fleet carry the Sheenway livery. A388XMC displays its Sheenway livery in this Parliament Square scene in July 1994. Of note is the former Midland Fox fleet number 231, a throwback to when TGM was part of that organisation. Colin Lloyd

One of two coaches in the Tellings Golden Miller fleet to carry this special Gulliver's Travel Agency livery, F807TMD is a Van Hool Alizee bodied Volvo B10M. Kentish Bus also use dedicated coaches for GTA, but theirs carry an all white livery. New in 1989, it is carrying a load of visitors when entering Oxford Street from Marble Arch in August 1994. Colin Lloyd

Edward Thomas & Son operate an almost exclusive fleet of British built products with mostly AEC and Leyland chassis and Plaxton bodies. Typifying this welcome trend is 267PPH, a Leyland Leopard with Plaxton Supreme IV body in the West Ewell yard during September 1994 having completed an earlier school contract duty.
Geoff Rixon

THORPES

F.E.Thorpe & Sons Ltd, 272 Latimer Road, London, W10 6QY

NMJ281V	Volvo B58-56	Plaxton Supreme IV	C49F	1980	Ex Horseshoe, Kempston, 1991
✗ KNP3X	Volvo B10M-56	Plaxton Viewmaster IV Express	C45F	1982	Ex Goldliner, Droitwich, 1983
C118EMG	Volvo B10M-61	Plaxton Paramount 3200 II	C48FT	1985	Ex Horseshoe, Kempston, 1991
D676BRY	Freight Rover Sherpa 350D	Whittaker	C16FL	1986	Ex Winson, Loughborough, 1990
D865OEJ	Renault Master T35D	Holdsworth	C14F	1987	Ex McCarthy, Cross Inn, 1989
E157KDP	Volvo B10M-61	Plaxton Paramount 3500 III	C49FT	1987	Ex Ralph's, Langley, 1994
E29WGJ	Mercedes-Benz 709D	Pilcher Green	C18FL	1987	Ex Police Convalescent Home, 1987
E914NEW	Volkswagen LT55	Optare City Pacer	B25F	1988	Ex Viscount, 1993
E915NEW	Volkswagen LT55	Optare City Pacer	B25F	1988	Ex Viscount, 1993
E916NEW	Volkswagen LT55	Optare City Pacer	B25F	1988	Ex Viscount, 1993
E917NEW	Volkswagen LT55	Optare City Pacer	B25F	1988	Ex Viscount, 1993
E217RDW	Leyland Tiger TRCTL11/3ARZ	Plaxton Paramount 3500 III	C51FT	1988	Ex Hill, Tredegar, 1993
E638TWW	Volkswagen LT55	Optare City Pacer	B12FL	1988	Ex London Buses, 1992
E998TWU	Volkswagen LT55	Optare City Pacer	B12FL	1988	Ex London Buses, 1992
E999TWU	Volkswagen LT55	Optare City Pacer	B12FL	1988	Ex London Buses, 1992
G892PGU	Leyland-DAF 400	Carlyle	C14FL	1989	Ex Ex Link Line, Littlehampton, 1993
G822UMU	Volvo B10M-61	Plaxton Paramount 3500 III	C53F	1989	
J839KNL	Leyland-DAF 400	Autobus Classique	C16F	1992	Ex Jones, Newton Aycliffe, 1994
K2FET	Mercedes-Benz 709D	Alexander (Belfast) AM	B14FL	1993	
K3FET	Mercedes-Benz 709D	Alexander (Belfast) AM	B14FL	1993	
K4FET	Mercedes-Benz 814D	Plaxton Beaver	C33F	1993	

Previous Registration
E157KDP   WSV479

Livery
Yellow and white.

Special Livery
LRT Stationlink (Red and yellow) :- K2/3 FET

TIME TRAVEL

Time Travel London Ltd, 19 Nursery Road, Thornton Heath, Surrey, CR7 8RE

MLL952	AEC Regal IV	Metro-Cammell	B39F	1952	Ex preservation, 1992
RCN701	AEC Routemaster 2R2RH	Park Royal	H41/31F	1964	Ex Ashton (Non PSV), Ashtead, 1992
NMY628E	AEC Routemaster R2RH/2	Park Royal	H32/24F	1967	Ex London Buses, 1994
NMY637E	AEC Routemaster R2RH/2	Park Royal	H32/24F	1967	Ex North Mymms, Potters Bar, 1992
YKJ196	Volvo B58-56	Plaxton Supreme IV	C53F	1979	Ex North Mymms, Potters Bar, 19920
BBB532V	Bedford VAS5	Plaxton Supreme IV	C29F	1980	Ex Dobbins, London N11, 1994
SIB6176	Van Hool T815	Van Hool Acron	C48FT	1982	Ex Reed, Kingsley, 1993
FNM727Y	Ford Transit	Trimoco	M12	1982	Ex Kimlon, London NW10, 1993
✗ EUI4415	Volvo B10M-61	Berkhof Everest 370	C49FT	1983	Ex Hambridge, Nuneaton, 1994
VJR248	Volvo B10M-61	Van Hool Astral	CH49/9FT	1984	Ex Admiral, Hemel Hempstead, 1993
LSU783	Volvo B10M-53	Van Hool Astral 3	CH47/11FT	1984	Ex Harvey, Harlow, 1994
D212OKJ	Ford Transit	Ford	M11	1986	Ex GP Travel, London N5, 1991
D909XMV	Ford Transit	Coachcraft	M12	1986	Ex Finlan, Cookham Dean, 1991
NMC528	Leyland Tiger TRCTL11/3RZ	Duple 320	C50FT	1987	Ex Limebourne, London SW8, 1994
D374SNS	Freight Rover Sherpa 350D	Scott	C16F	1987	Ex Lutonian, Luton, 1991
191TPH	Freight Rover Sherpa 350D	Scott	C16F	1987	Ex Wood, Handsworth, 1991
E315OPR	Volvo B10M-61	Van Hool Alizee	C53F	1988	Ex Dodds, Troon, 1993
F635HVM	Mazda E2200	Made To Measure	M14	1989	Ex GP Travel, London N5, 1991
NMC785	MAN 16.290	Jonckheere Deauville P599	C51FT	1989	Ex North Mymms, Potters Bar, 1992
M370LJA	LDV 400	LDV	B16F	1994	
M380LJA	LDV 400	LDV	B16F	1994	

Previous registrations

191TPH	D385SNS	NMC528	D134HML	SIB6176	FKX238Y, ROF882, 9740EL
EUI4415	BDV862Y	NMC785	F915YNV	VJR248	A621UGD
LSU783	A547XUH	RCN701	From New	YKJ196	JBX693X
MLL952	From New				

Livery
Blue and white.

TRAVELLERS

Brelaton Ltd, Unit C1 Tamian Way, Hounslow, Middx, TW4 6BL

H433GVL	Kassbohrer Setra S215HR	Kassbohrer Rational	C53F	1991
H434GVL	Kassbohrer Setra S215HR	Kassbohrer Rational	C53F	1991
H435GVL	Kassbohrer Setra S215HR	Kassbohrer Rational	C53F	1991
H2TCC	Kassbohrer Setra S215HD	Kassbohrer Tornado	C49FT	1991
H5TCC	Toyota Coaster HDB30R	Caetano Optimo II	C18F	1991
H6TCC	Toyota Coaster HDB30R	Caetano Optimo II	C18F	1991
H7TCC	Toyota Coaster HDB30R	Caetano Optimo II	C18F	1991
J8TCC	MAN 10.180	Jonckheere Deauville P35	C28FT	1991
J9TCC	MAN 10.180	Jonckheere Deauville P35	C28FT	1991
J1TCC	Kassbohrer Setra S215HD	Kassbohrer Tornado	C49FT	1992
J3TCC	Kassbohrer Setra S215HD	Kassbohrer Tornado	C49FT	1992
J4TCC	Kassbohrer Setra S215HD	Kassbohrer Tornado	C49FT	1992
J5TCC	Kassbohrer Setra S215HD	Kassbohrer Tornado	C49FT	1992
J6TCC	Kassbohrer Setra S215HD	Kassbohrer Tornado	C49FT	1992
K2JTB	Kassbohrer Setra S215HD	Kassbohrer Tornado	C53F	1992
K1TCC	Kassbohrer Setra S215HD	Kassbohrer Tornado	C28FT	1992
K20TCC	Kassbohrer Setra S215HD	Kassbohrer Tornado	C49FT	1994
K30TCC	Kassbohrer Setra S215HD	Kassbohrer Tornado	C49FT	1994
K40TCC	Kassbohrer Setra S215HD	Kassbohrer Tornado	C49FT	1994
K50TCC	Kassbohrer Setra S215HD	Kassbohrer Tornado	C49FT	1994
K60TCC	Kassbohrer Setra S215HD	Kassbohrer Tornado	C49FT	1994
L1TCC	Volvo B10M-62	Plaxton Premiere 350 II	C49FT	1994
L2TCC	Volvo B10M-62	Plaxton Premiere 350 II	C49FT	1994
L3TCC	Volvo B10M-60	Plaxton Premiere 350	C53F	1994
L4TCC	Volvo B10M-62	Plaxton Premiere 350 II	C53F	1994
L5TCC	Volvo B10M-62	Plaxton Premiere 350 II	C53F	1994
L6TCC	Volvo B10M-62	Plaxton Premiere 350 II	C53F	1994
L7TCC	Volvo B10M-62	Plaxton Premiere 350 II	C53F	1994
L8TCC	Volvo B10M-62	Plaxton Premiere 320 II	C57F	1994
L9TCC	Volvo B10M-62	Plaxton Premiere 320 II	C57F	1994
L10TCC	Volvo B10M-62	Plaxton Premiere 320 II	C57F	1994
M10TCC	Volvo B12R	Jonckheere Monaco	CH57/14CT	1994

Previous registrations

H2TCC	H809GFW	J8TCC	J1TCC
J1TCC	J7TCC	J9TCC	J2TCC

Named Vehicle;
K1TCC   The Diplomat

Livery
Silver with red, white and blue relief.

TRINATOURS LTD

Trina Tours Ltd, 152a Shaftesbury Avenue, London, WC2.

E975NMK	Volvo B10M-61	Plaxton Paramount 3500 III	C53F	1988
K810EET	Volvo B10M-60	Van Hool Alizee HE	C31FT	1992
K704RNR	Toyota Coaster HDB30R	Caetano Optimo II	C18F	1992
K420JWB	Volvo B10M-60	Van Hool Alizee HE	C53F	1993
K592VBC	MAN 10.190	Caetano Algarve II	C35F	1993
K593VBC	MAN 10.190	Caetano Algarve II	C35F	1993

Livery
Silver and black.

Nestling within the mini/midibuses and coaches of the Thorpes fleet are six full size coaches. Probably the most interesting is this relatively rare example of the Plaxton Viewmaster on the ubiquitous Volvo B10M. Also of note is the fitment of a two piece door, most Viewmasters having the single piece type. Crossing Putney Bridge in August 1994 is KNP3X. Colin Lloyd

Crossing Buckingham Palace Road in June 1994 is Time Travel's EUI4415, a Berkhof bodied Volvo B10M. This high floor example carries the less common Everest type body, the Esprite style being more popular with the majority of British operators. Colin Lloyd

Typifying the trend towards the use of select DVLC registrations, most of the Travellers stock now carry these marks. L3TCC is no exception seen in Trafalgar Square passing the National Gallery. One of ten examples delivered in 1994, this one was the only example of the Volvo B10M-60 with original Plaxton Premiere body, the others being B10M-62s with the Premiere II bodywork. P.J. Stockwell

A quiet Sunday morning in a normally bustling Regent Street finds the latest addition to the pristine Travellers fleet, M10TCC. Another unique vehicle within these pages, it is a Jonckheere Monaco atop the equally new Volvo B12M chassis. M10TCC is a seventy one seater, basically a double deck version of the popular Jonckheere Deauville. P.J. Stockwell

Travellers use three of their vehicles in a dedicated livery for the Japanese Tourist Board (JTB). The smallest of the three is this MAN 10.180 with Jonckheere Deauville P35 minicoach body. The Embankment near Waterloo Bridge provides the setting in April 1994. Colin Lloyd

One of the newer vehicles in the modest yet modern Trinatours fleet is K592VBC. With Caetano Algarve II coachwork on the MAN 10.190 chassis, its body is recognisable from earlier Algarve variants by virtue of the curved up sweep of the windscreen. Having earned pole position at the lights in Parliament Square, it awaits the green light in November 1994. Colin Lloyd

WESTBUS

Westbus (UK) Ltd, 27a Spring Grove Road, Hounslow, Middx. TW3 4BE

NNS235V	Ford R1114	Plaxton Supreme IV	C53F	1979	Ex Swinard, Ashford, 1986
D101BNV	Volvo B10M-61	Jonckheere Jubilee P599	C49FT	1987	
D102BNV	Volvo B10M-61	Jonckheere Jubilee P599	C49FT	1987	
D103BNV	Volvo B10M-53	Jonckheere Jubilee P95	CH49/12FT	1987	
D104BNV	Volvo B10M-53	Jonckheere Jubilee P95	CH49/12FT	1987	
D105BNV	Volvo B10M-53	Jonckheere Jubilee P95	CH49/12FT	1987	
F906YNV	Volvo B10M-60	Jonckheere Deauville P599	C49FT	1989	
F994UME	Volvo B10M-60	Duple 340	C36FT	1989	
F995UME	Volvo B10M-60	Duple 340	C53F	1989	
F996UME	Volvo B10M-60	Duple 340	C53F	1989	
H176EJF	Toyota Coaster HDB30R	Caetano Optimo II	C18F	1991	
K508WNR	Volvo B10M-60	Jonckheere Deauville P599	C51FT	1993	
K509WNR	Volvo B10M-60	Jonckheere Deauville P599	C51FT	1993	

Livery
Red and cream with black relief.

WEST'S COACHES LTD

West's Coaches Ltd, 198-200 High Road, Woodford Bridge, Essex, IG8 9EF

JFP177V	Ford R1114	Duple Dominant II	C53F	1980	
LUE260V	Ford R1114	Duple Dominant II	C46F	1980	
KGA56Y	Bova EL26/581	Bova Europa	C53F	1982	Ex Crawford, Neilston, 1987
A15BUS	Bova EL28/581	Duple Calypso	C53F	1982	Ex Crawford, Neilston, 1987
A14BUS	Bova EL26/581	Duple Calypso	C53F	1984	Ex Antler, Rugeley, 1988
A16BUS	Volvo B10M-60	Plaxton Paramount 3500 III	C53F	1989	Ex Park's, Hamilton, 1992
A12BUS	DAF SB2305DHS585	Caetano Algarve	C53F	1989	Ex Traject, Halifax, 1991
A13BUS	TAZ D3200	TAZ Dubrava	C53F	1989	
A19BUS	DAF SB3000DKV601	Caetano Algarve	C49FT	1989	Ex Ace, Mansfield, 1989
A18BUS	Volvo B10M-60	Plaxton Paramount 3500 III	C53F	1989	Ex Essex Coachways, London E2, 1994
F814TMD	Volvo B10M-60	Plaxton Paramount 3500 III	C53F	1989	Ex Lacey, London E6, 1994

Previous Registrations

A12BUS	F233RJX	A15BUS	A321HFP	A18BUS	F813TMD
A13BUS	F788TBC	A16BUS	F972HGE	A19BUS	G949VBC
A14BUS	B127DHL				

Livery
White with red, orange and yellow relief.

WESTWAY

D.J. West, 1 Belmont Road, Belmont, Surrey, SM2 6DW

GSU387	Volvo B10M-61	Plaxton Paramount 3500	C53F	1984	Ex Essex Coachways, London E3, 1992
B111CCS	Volvo B10M-61	Jonkheere Jubilee P599	C53F	1985	Ex Jenkins, Skewen, 1990
C515BFB	Ford Transit 190D	Dormobile	B16F	1985	Ex Badgerline, 1994
C532BHY	Ford Transit 190D	Dormobile	B16F	1986	Ex Badgerline, 1994
C521BFB	Ford Transit 190D	Dormobile	B16F	1986	Ex Badgerline, 1994
D29RKX	Volvo B10M-61	Jonkheere Jubilee P599	C49F	1987	Ex Cantabrica, Watford, 1993
F981HGE	Volvo B10M-60	Plaxton Paramount 3500 III	C53F	1989	Ex Fuggles, Benenden, 1994
L961CAY	Toyota Coaster HZB50R	Caetano Optimo II	C21F	1994	

Previous Registration
GSU387   A380XMC

Livery
White with navy blue and red relief.

WINDSORIAN

Windsorian Coaches Ltd, 103 Arthur Road, Windsor, Berks, SL4 1RU

PPG4R	Bedford YMT	Plaxton Supreme III	C53F	1977	Ex King, Kirkcowan, 1984
x797ONU	Volvo B58-56	Plaxton Viewmaster IV	C53F	1979	
635UNU	Volvo B58-56	Plaxton Viewmaster IV	C53F	1979	
LOU437Y	Bedford YNT	Plaxton Supreme IV	C53F	1982	Ex Bowers, Bridgend, 1985
FTL738	Volvo B10M-61	Plaxton Paramount 3500	C49FT	1983	Ex Pugsley, Yeo Vale, 1992
UTA119	Volvo B10M-61	Berkhof Esprite 350	C49FT	1983	Ex Heard, Hartland, 1994
A188OOT	Mercedes-Benz L608D	Robin Hood	C19F	1984	
SSU503	BedfordYNT	Plaxton Paramount 3200	C53F	1984	
LIW3221	Volvo B10M-61	Caetano Algarve	C49FT	1986	Ex Patterson, Birmingham, 1994
C30PRX	Leyland Tiger TRCTL11/3R	Plaxton Paramount 3500 II	C53F	1986	
D141YMO	Bedford YMP	Plaxton Paramount 3200 III	C35F	1987	
E200FCF	Volvo B10M-61	Ikarus Blue Danube	C49FT	1987	
G226DGM	Mercedes-Benz 814D	Phoenix	C24F	1989	

Previous Registrations

797ONU	YJB332T	FTL738	FUA380Y	SSU503		A511CAN
635UNU	YJB333T	LIW3221	C705KDS	UTA119		JVW158Y

Livery
White with dark blue and red relief.

WINGS EXECUTIVE TRAVEL / ALLIED

Wings Luxury Travel Ltd, 126-127 Waterloo Road, Uxbridge, Middx. UB8 2QZ
Allied Coachlines Ltd, 126-127 Waterloo Road, Uxbridge, Middx. UB8 2QZ

Wings Fleet

WLT798	Ford Transit	Coachcraft	C16F	1989
WLT289	Ford Transit	Coachcraft	C16F	1989
WLT982	Ford Transit	Deansgate	M12	1989
WET590	Mercedes-Benz 811D	Optare StarRider	C16FT	1990
x WET859	Mercedes-Benz 811D	Optare StarRider	C16FT	1990
WET476	MAN 10.180	Caetano Algarve	C28FT	1992
WET725	MAN 10.180	Caetano Algarve	C28FT	1992
WLT746	Mercedes-Benz 814D	Optare StarRider	C29F	1993
L860DPK	Mercedes-Benz 814D	Optare StarRider	C20FT	1994
M928TYG	Mercedes-Benz 814D	Optare StarRider	C29F	1994
M929TYG	Mercedes-Benz 814D	Optare StarRider	C29F	1994

Allied Fleet

WLU887	DAF SB2305DHS585	Caetano Algarve	C53F	1989	Ex Anderson, London SE1, 1993
KBG520	DAF SB2305DHS585	Caetano Algarve	C53F	1989	Ex Tate, Markyate, 1994
FRG714	DAF SB2305DHS585	Jonckheere Deauville P599	C51FT	1989	Ex Godson, Cross Gates, 1994
RSU294	DAF SB2305DHS585	Duple 340	C53FT	1989	Ex Brewers, 1994
206EJO	DAF SB2305DHS585	Caetano Algarve	C53F	1990	Ex Spanish Speaking, London NW1, 1994
TFY241	DAF SB2305DHS585	Caetano Algarve	C53F	1990	Ex Spanish Speaking, London NW1, 1994
SNR930	TAZ D3200	TAZ Dubrava	C53F	1990	Ex Eurobus, Harmondsworth, 1991
J461NJU	DAF MB230LB615	Caetano Algarve	C49FT	1992	
J462NJU	DAF MB230LB615	Caetano Algarve	C49FT	1992	
J463NJU	DAF MB230LB615	Caetano Algarve	C49FT	1992	

Previous Registrations

206EJO	G916WAY	WET476	J513LRY	WLT746		L835MWT
FRG714	G471GNH	WET590	G695BLO	WLT798		F377EHE
KBG520	F423RRY, WIJ297, F960RGS	WET725	J514LRY	WLT982		G210YLD
RSU294	G400JEP	WET859	G699BLO	WLU887		F194PNR
SNR930	G576WUT	WLT289	F474EHE			
TFY241	G917WAY					

Liveries
Wings: White with red, orange and yellow relief.
Allied: White with blue relief. (G577WUT is Blue with white relief).

Special Liveries
Eurolines (White with red and blue fleetnames): FRG714, WLU887, J461-463NJU
Visitors Sightseeing (White with red, yellow and black fleetnames): 206EJO & TFY241.

Above **Westbus (UK) of Hounslow** is a subsidiary of Westbus PTY, Australia's largest bus and coach operator. The British operation caters mainly for incoming tourist work although British and continental work is also undertaken. A typical private hire to Brighton finds Duple 340 bodied Volvo B10M F996UME in the summer sunshine. Malcolm King

Centre **Representing one of the high specification coaches** used by Westbus is this impressive Jonckheere Jubilee P95 bodied on the Volvo B10M-53 chassis. One of three such vehicles in the fleet, note the rear lower saloon seating well. Hanworth Road Hampton finds D104BNV undertaking a school contract duty in September 1994.

Left **By far the smallest vehicle** in the Westbus operation is this Caetano Optimo II bodied Toyota Coaster. With a mere eighteen seats, H176EJF is used predominantly on private hires as shown in this view taken in Parliament Square in October 1994. Colin Lloyd

Another rarity in this book, this time a Bova with the Duple Calypso body. A short lived product built in collaboration with Bova, it was basically a low height version of the Duple Caribbean. One of two such examples in the West's of Woodford fleet, A14BUS carries a select registration along with the majority of the coaches owned. F. Lawrance

The coaches operated by Westway of Belmont Surrey never fail to catch the eye by virtue of their unusual livery design. This view in St.Margaret Street, Westminster shows D29RKX, a Jonckheere Jubilee P599 bodied Volvo B10M in June 1994. Colin Lloyd

Windsorian have a pair of Plaxton Viewmasters in the fleet, both on Volvo B58 chassis. Parked under the trees in Park Lane by the side of Hyde Park is 797ONU, bought new in 1979 although subsequently re-registered from a T suffix plate. Colin Lloyd

Wings Executive Travel operate a fleet of minicoaches, many being of high specification with tables, toilets and air conditioning. Complete with select registration, WET859 typifies the luxury afforded to this Optare StarRider when photographed at Hampton Court in May 1994. Geoff Rixon

WOOLLONS COACHES

R.D. Woollon, Falcon Estate, North Feltham Trading Estate, Central Way, North Feltham, Middx. TW14 6XJ

ESK807	Leyland Leopard PSU3E/4R	Duple Dominant II	C46F	1978	Ex John, Kenfig Hill, 1991
EPM135V	AEC Reliance 6U2R	Duple Dominant II Express	C53F	1979	Ex Smith-Ivins, High Wycombe, 1993
RSU883	Bedford YNT	Duple Dominant IV Express	C53F	1982	Ex Martlew, Barry, 1990
C270GOF	Freight-Rover Sherpa 350D	Chassis Developments	C16F	1986	Ex Ellis, Kelvedon, 1993
C855VRY	MAN MT8.136	G C Smith Whippett	C28F	1986	Ex Hudson, Downley, 1991
D930LYC	Bedford Venturer YNV	Duple 320	C57F	1987	Ex Sanders, Holt, 1994
E861TNG	Bedford Venturer YNV	Duple 320	C57F	1988	Ex Sanders, Holt, 1994
F864SPC	Volkswagen Kombi	Devon Conversions	M11	1989	Ex Epsom Coaches, 1993

Previous Registrations
ESK807 UWA98S RSU883 PNT832X

Livery
White, caramel and dark brown.

One of the last variants of the Duple Dominant design was the MkVI version. An example of this body is RSU883, the sole Bedford YNT in the fleet of Woollens Coaches of Heathrow. Seen departing Lady Eleanor Holles School in Hampton on a warm October day in 1994. Geoff Rixon